High-er Help

How Businesses Use Experts to Shortcut Growth, Improvement & Capacity

BRANDY LAWSON, MBA

HIGH-ER HELP

How Businesses Use Experts to Shortcut Growth, Improvement & Capacity

Book Design by
Transcendent Publishing
TranscendentPublishing.com

Author Photo by: Karianne Mundstadt

ISBN: 979-8-9885147-9-4

Printed in the United States of America.

This book is dedicated to those courageous enough
to run a business.

We are a special kind of crazy & bold.

Contents

Contents

What to Expect from This Book

The intention of this book is to help ignite the possibilities of using the expertise of others to make running your business a more enjoyable experience.

Each one of us has our own unique set of skills and talents, areas where we truly shine and thrive. These unique traits are our genius, the fuel behind our ability to make a difference in the world. But to truly harness this potential, it requires recognition that we can't do it alone.

Whether you're molding a masterpiece from clay, crafting heartfelt verses, coding the next world-changing software, or delivering top-notch salon services, the magic doesn't stop at creation. It's about reaching the right people and delivering your unique genius in a way that they can integrate into their lives. This is where the expertise of others come into play, serving as a force multiplier that allows you to harness your genius to its maximum potential. By leveraging the skills of experts, you're not just extending your reach—you're also saving your time and energy, allowing you to be present and engaged in every aspect of your life.

Are you in?

If you thought "great," exclaimed aloud, or even thought, "yeah right," then read on! Both enthusiasts and skeptics will find value ahead.

When we speak of an "expert," what comes to mind? A specialist with advanced knowledge, a professional with a particular set of skills, or an individual with a deep understanding in a specific field? Yes, all of these.

But in the context of this book, we take it a step further.

> An 'expert' is someone who leverages their in-depth knowledge and specialized skills to help a business grow, improve, and add capacity.

They range from professionals hired by businesses—like a bookkeeper, HR consultant, or a marketing agency—to personal growth facilitators like a personal trainer, life coach, or executive coach.

> Expertise makes something complex appear simple and intelligible. Bullshit makes something simple appear unnecessarily complex and unintelligible.
>
> Expertise creates value for people who don't know better. Bullshit extracts value from people who don't know better.
>
> – Mark Manson

In my own journey, I've had firsthand experience with the pivotal role of experts. The first two years of my business I was a solo performer, a one-woman army. I thought I could do it all myself and deliver brilliance and quality unmatched by anyone else. Yes, please insert your eyeroll here. I soon realized that my ever-growing list of important, then urgent, tasks—invoicing, following up on unpaid invoices, bookkeeping, taxes, and marketing my own business—kept piling up. It was a classic case of procrastination fueled by fear and the discomfort of performing tasks I wasn't skilled at. I was drowning and needed help, or there wouldn't be a business to run.

This led me to hire my first expert, a business coach. I'll admit I wasn't the easiest client. I resisted change, argued, and was reluctant to address the root cause of my problems. But with time, perseverance, and a lot of nagging, I started to address those scary tasks and developed habits to keep my brain from sabotaging my business.

This experience taught me two things:

1. the power of accountability and

2. the value of trusting and following an expert's advice without overthinking it or trying to make it my own too soon.

I was quickly able to put this knowledge to work.

My business initially centered around building websites for clients. Just three projects in, I recognized a problem. Most business owners didn't really know what they needed from a website. If I relied on their guidance, the website wouldn't add any value to their business. This realization shifted my role from just a website builder to an expert, guiding clients through the process of uncovering the essential role their website plays in their business.

The same struggle extends to many other experts.

We have in-depth skills and knowledge, but there is often a gap between our understanding and our clients'. This disconnect can lead to miscommunication, inefficiency, and missed opportunities for growth.

This is where this book comes in. It's designed to bridge this gap. If you're a client, this book will prepare you to be a better one. You'll learn how to work with experts in a way that maximizes your return on investment. If you're an expert, you'll discover how to meet your clients where they are, prepare them to extract the most value from your service, and deliver your service effectively to help them grow, improve, or add capacity.

In essence, this book serves as a guide for better engagement and results. It's not just about transactional relationships between clients and experts. It's about creating partnerships that fuel growth, improvement, and added capacity. It's about acknowledging our limits, seeking help, and leveraging each other's strengths. As we journey together, you'll find this book to be helpful and approachable, and yes, even a bit quirky, reflecting the ups, downs, and all-around adventurous nature of working with experts.

As we know, nothing in life is guaranteed, including working with experts (as you no doubt have experienced). However, there are specific steps to take and ways to set yourself, and your expert, up to get your desired outcomes (a.k.a. success). I've learned these lessons the hard way, and by reading this book you have the opportunity to learn them the easy way.

In short, you can use experts to:

- Accelerate knowledge

- Build bridges between where you are and where you want to be

- Show you what you don't know (a.k.a. the gaps that need to be filled) to overcome the Dunning-Kruger effect (More on that later)

- Make things easier (they know the road)

- Get sh*t done (they complete projects or tasks outside your skillset)

- Get back time, energy, and resources (In other words, they add capacity)

- Make things more predictable

- Amplify your impact

Long story short, experts = leverage.

And leverage = doing more with less.

I feel like we could all use more of that.

But to be fair, experts can also be an incredible time and energy suck if they aren't a fit. Which is why I'm not going to gloss over the hard truths and pitfalls of hiring in this book. We'll get nitty gritty into the good, the bad, and the ugly.

If you're ready for the journey, then let's get started.

PART I:

Base Camp

When you choose to collaborate with experts, you're making a strategic decision to relinquish some control—not out of weakness, but out of wisdom. You're understanding the limitations of your current resources and embracing the power of diverse expertise.

Working with experts is about harnessing their experience, their unique insights, and their specialized skills to accelerate your business' growth. It's recognizing that the business landscape, like any terrain, be it mountain or water, has its complexities and having an expert guide can be invaluable.

This isn't about losing your leadership. On the contrary, it's about strengthening it.

Every expert you bring in elevates your team's capabilities, enhancing your business' ability to withstand challenges and seize opportunities.

Crucially, this collaboration is anchored in trust. You're trusting in their proficiency, their knowledge, and their ability to deliver results. It's like delegating a critical task to a trusted team member, freeing up your time and energy to focus on the big picture.

In essence, working with experts demands a mindset of collaboration, trust, and humility. It's about leading your business towards success with a firm belief in collective wisdom. And let's be honest, that's a strategy we could all get behind.

Chapter One

Why Hire Experts

I f we imagine your business is a ship and you are the captain, here are some of the ways that experts can help.

First off, experts are your ship's supercharged engines. Their knowledge and experience can thrust your ship full steam ahead, leaving competitors bobbing in your wake. They help you accelerate your knowledge and steer clear of the stormy seas of confusion.

When it comes to navigating these waters, consider your expert as the lighthouse that guides your ship from the rocky shores of your current situation to the safe harbor of where you want to be. They illuminate the path, making it easier for you to traverse even the most tumultuous waters.

Ever heard of a ship setting sail without a map? Neither have I. And that's where the Dunning-Kruger effect comes in. The Dunning-Kruger effect is a psychological principle coined by David Dunning and Justin Kruger. It basically describes a cognitive bias where people with relatively low ability at a task overestimate their own ability, and conversely, people with high ability at a task underestimate their competence.

You may have seen this at work, or experienced it yourself when new to a skill or task. Initially, you might feel a surge of confidence, thinking you've mastered it after achieving only a basic understanding. This is the first part of the Dunning-Kruger effect - the 'peak of Mount Stupid', as it's often called.

However, as we gain more knowledge and experience, we start to realize the depth and complexity of the skill, and our self-perception of competence drops, sometimes excessively. This is the second part of the Dunning-Kruger effect - the 'valley of despair'.

Essentially, this concept illustrates how our perception of our abilities can often be at odds with reality, and it serves as a good reminder of the value of continuous learning and self-assessment.

Like a captain overestimating his skills, it's easy to sail right into a maelstrom if you don't know where you're heading. Luckily, your expert, with their wealth of knowledge, can help you navigate around these pitfalls.

They also know the sea lanes better than any old salt. Whether it's avoiding whirlpools of inefficiency or riding the trade winds of opportunity, they can make your voyage significantly easier. They've sailed these waters before and know all the tricks to make it smooth sailing.

Need the sails adjusted or the deck swabbed? Your expert isn't just about giving orders; they pitch in and get sh*t done. From tying the perfect sailor's knot to keeping morale high during stormy weather, they've got your back.

With these seasoned sailors aboard, you're no longer both captain and crew. They give back time, energy, and resources by taking on tasks that would otherwise drain your capacity. Suddenly, you have time to plot the course and focus on steering the ship.

Sailing the seas can be unpredictable, but with an expert crew your ship's journey becomes less about dodging rogue waves and more about enjoying the smooth sail. They've got the weather updates, the star charts, and the instincts to make the voyage as predictable as possible.

Last, but certainly not least, with a crew of experts on board your ship makes a bigger splash. Your impact on the market is like the wake of your ship—larger, more powerful, and turning heads wherever you go.

So, experts are like your ship's trusty crew. The leverage you need in your business voyage. They help you do more with less: less floundering, less going around in circles, less walking the plank.

Why Hire Experts: Growth

On paper, pretty much anything seems doable. Build a desk? Sure! Remodel a bathroom? They do it on TV, how hard can it be? Quantum Physics? YouTube it!

But then when information needs to turn into action, the full impact of the unknown becomes apparent. Sometimes the unknown shows up as a stubbed toe or a stumble, or sometimes as a trip to the emergency room after an amateur encounter with a skill saw (I've never seen that part when they do it on TV).

One of the key problems with growth is that we humans tend to overestimate our knowledge & capabilities in new areas. Basically, you don't know what you don't know.

An academic sidebar here, the not knowing what you don't know concept has a name: it's called the Dunning-Kruger effect. Yeah, humans have such substantial experience with this that researchers studied it enough to give it a name.

To get real fancy, we can say it is a cognitive bias. That is, it's an error in our thinking—usually a result of our brain trying to simplify information processing. And that is helpful for us, until it isn't.

When an organization is growing or wants to grow, it's just not possible to do everything yourself. I feel confident stating this as a fact because I tried, and I've worked with dozens of other business owners who have tried, and failed.

More often than not, the people or teams tasked with spearheading growth don't even have enough capacity to handle all the must-do tasks, never mind putting together a strategic plan to guide the work or explore new channels and tactics for growth.

What to do? Stay stuck in the overwhelm, under-resourced, and stressed-out growth and panic cycle, or try another way? Choosing the other way is why you hire an expert.

Growth is messy. We can feel our way through it, falling into the pitfalls, taking unintended routes, wandering off the path, and then finding our way back.

The hard way is one way to learn; academics call that primary research. And sometimes we need the lesson via primary research, or at least I do. But not always. The hard way isn't the only path to success.

Shortcuts Instead of Scenic Routes

Hiring and working with experts helps smooth the path and lets you take shortcuts instead of scenic routes on your way to growth, making it all feel less hard, exhausting, & lonely.

Hiring experts can help counteract the errors in your thinking and show you what you don't know you don't know before it becomes a serious situation. The right expert is your expedition guide in the new world you find yourself in, being your sherpa to find the most direct path to growth. Using experts in this way keeps you and your team doing the things you are brilliant at and builds the knowledge base required to extend your capabilities.

Leveraging an expert for growth means less wandering, wondering and guessing, and more progress, strategy, and execution. It means helping your team achieve objectives, but also "leveling up" your internal systems and knowledge for the area.

When it comes to growth projects, it can really pay off to call in the cavalry of outside experts. If you only stick to your own crew, it's like spinning too many plates—sooner or later, something's got to give.

If you rely only on your existing team, growth projects might get shoved to the bottom of the to-do list, or your team might find themselves knee-deep in unknown territory (typically growth projects require new expertise). Even worse, you might end up spending your precious time and resources trying to learn skills that might never really pay off, rather than investing that energy into beefing up your business. So, let's not fall into the "do-it-yourself" trap, okay?

Why Hire Experts: Improvement

Looking for improvement areas is like taking a step back and squinting at your business from afar. You get to see the big picture, identifying bottlenecks and inefficiencies that have been slowing you down like a snail on a sticky trail. It's about clearing the clutter, streamlining the flow, and eliminating anything that doesn't contribute to creating a majestic masterpiece. Or, in business terms, delivering value to your customers.

And as business owners know, this isn't a one-time deal, like ripping off a bandage. Nope! Process and systems improvement is an ongoing saga, an adventure where you're constantly refining and tweaking.

And it is in these cases that people in the business have the opposite problem: Sometimes we know too much.

Have you ever done that annoying exercise where you have to instruct someone else how to make a peanut butter & jelly sandwich?

It's a reliable way to frustrate people.

Okay, so that's not the actual point of the exercise. But you already know the point of the experiment here. It shows us that no one successfully communicates to the other person on the first try with all the necessary information to complete a seemingly simple action.

This is the Curse of Knowledge, and why you hire experts to improve.

In the last section we talked about hiring an expert to help with growth because of the Dunning-Krueger effect—when you don't know what you don't know.

There's an opposite cognitive bias known as "The Curse of Knowledge."

This is where we can't see what we already know, and unknowingly assume that others have the background to understand. The peanut butter & jelly exercise is a terrific illustration of the Curse of Knowledge at work. What? Why would I have to tell you to open the loaf of bread??

So… sometimes we don't know what we don't know, and other times we don't know what we already know. Not knowing and too much knowing is dangerous, and in both cases, we need external perspective to counter our own perspective. Wow… isn't the human brain weird?

I'm sure you've been here—the place we really feel & see the Curse of Knowledge is when it comes to expanding our teams and improving our capabilities. Much like the peanut butter & jelly exercise, we tend to skip over parts or completely forget resources and context necessary to delegate or complete tasks.

But that's where experts can help.

> **Experts can help when improvement is needed because they have an outside perspective and can more clearly see the steps and context for tasks and systems. Plus, they usually have a system to evaluate & improve the system (it's very meta).**

Hiring experts can help you improve these 4 key areas:

1. **Remove bottlenecks.** Experts help here by being the pair of eyes you simply cannot be. They see the context. They see where the bottlenecks are happening and can help diagnose and triage the cause of bottlenecks.

2. **Expand capacity with more ease.** Experts have skills and expertise that it might take you months or years to acquire. They can not only take on work for you, but also help improve efficiency or create more effective processes and systems. Increasing output doesn't have to be a struggle.

3. **Track outcomes without micromanaging.** Better outcomes require better systems, and better systems means that we must talk about what's not working to make it better. No one looks forward to talking about what's not working, as that tends to devolve into a blame game featuring a lot of perspectives and feelings but no data. Experts can provide help in the form of defining key performance indicators (KPIs) and actual data, to eliminate the debate of opinions about if someone is doing their job, and instead use facts to track outcomes and gain insights for improvement.

4. **Enhance team performance.** A better-informed team is a better performing team. Knowledge distribution accelerates improvement, because when everyone has

access to the information, they can participate in making great decisions. Distribution of knowledge isn't just information, but also training and interactions with the information (e.g., FAQs).

Embracing the fact that the Curse of Knowledge exists can help you not rest on your laurels, believing that you already have all the answers. Instead, you'll be able to seek out blind spots in your processes, build systems to help smooth information flow, be more able to ask for the help and expertise needed, and give yourself a break when it is super frustrating to achieve that improvement you are striving for.

Remember that even a group of highly trained project managers still struggle with the peanut butter & jelly exercise. Our brains are made for efficiency, and that can mean overlooking parts of our expertise that are obvious to others.

Hiring the right expert to tackle improvement not only gets you tangible advancement, but also overcomes the lack of internal resources and time to focus on completing improvements.

Using external experts also helps speed up the process so you can experience the results of the improvements, because they were fully implemented (and didn't get deprioritized when they were partially complete).

Why Hire Experts: Capacity

We've all been there—juggling multiple tasks, deadlines looming, and a to-do list that's more intimidating than the tax code. The bitter truth is, in our pursuit of success and growth we often find ourselves running on a capacity treadmill. We are perpetually trying to do more, achieve more, with the same 24 hours at our disposal.

Let's face it, time is an entrepreneur's most precious, non-renewable resource. So, how do you manage it all without losing your marbles or your enthusiasm? The secret sauce is leveraging the power of experts.

The Virtue of Delegation: Getting Off the Hamster Wheel

When we talk about hiring experts, we're not just referring to professionals with a fancy title. We're talking about individuals who have mastered their craft, who live and breathe their field of expertise. They are the game changers who can empower you to step off that hamster wheel and finally start moving forward.

Hiring experts is about investing in people who can lend their expertise to grow, improve, or support your business. It's about creating capacity by freeing up your time, allowing you to focus on what you do best.

Remember, every time you say 'yes' to a task that is not in your wheelhouse, you're saying 'no' to something else. Every hour spent wrestling with website design or figuring out complex tax laws is an hour not spent strategizing, creating, and connecting with your customers.

Strategic Capacity Creation: More Than Just Time Management

Now, don't mistake this for a lesson in time management. We're not just talking about squeezing more tasks into your day.

It's about strategic capacity creation.

Hiring an expert doesn't just get tasks off your plate, it brings in fresh perspective, innovative ideas, and specialized skill sets that you might not possess. It's about understanding the value of your time and maximizing it by delegating tasks to experts who can do them more efficiently and effectively.

Imagine having a social media expert curating your online presence, an HR consultant smoothing out team dynamics, or a bookkeeper ensuring your finances are in top-notch order. Suddenly, you're not just the CEO, you're the conductor of a well-orchestrated symphony, each expert playing their part to perfection.

The Invisible Payoff: Mental Space

One hidden benefit of hiring experts is the mental space it opens up. Delegating tasks to others reduces the cognitive load you carry. This newfound mental space can be channeled into thinking strategically, exploring new ideas, or even just taking a break for some much-needed self-care.

> **Remember, growth isn't just about pushing harder, it's about thinking smarter. And to think smarter you need space to breathe, to reflect, to strategize. Hiring experts provides you with just that.**

The Cost of Not Investing in Capacity

It's essential to view hiring experts through the lens of an investment, not an expense. Consider the long-term ROI from engaging a top-notch bookkeeper, marketing wizard, or HR guru.

And equally consider the cost of not investing in this additional capacity. The cost of missed opportunities, burnout, or mishandled tasks. The cost of staying stuck in the cycle of 'busyness' without tangible progress. Hiring experts helps you break free from this cycle, setting the stage for sustainable growth.

In essence, capacity isn't about doing more. It's about doing better. It's about recognizing where your genius lies and bringing in other geniuses to handle the rest. It's about evolving from a jack of all trades to a master of your trade.

As we wrap up this section, let's take a moment to reflect. Growth, improvement, capacity. Three compelling reasons to start hiring experts. By now you've probably realized that these aren't standalone benefits. They're interconnected threads of the same tapestry.

Next, we'll dive into the nuts and bolts of how to hire experts. But before we do, here's your nudge to embrace the concept of capacity. Consider it your permission slip to delegate, your invitation to stop spinning all the plates.

Chapter Two

How to Know
When to Hire Experts

I 've come to believe that, in both business and life, there's never a perfect time for anything. Planning to get married? Never a perfect time. Want to have a baby? Never a perfect time. Going to move, quit your job, get a new job, start a business? Never a perfect time.

Why do I know this? That's because I got fired, started a business, and had our son in 2012, none of which was planned and at that moment looked like the worst timing. It wasn't.

It's the same when you are ready to hire an expert.

There's never a perfect time to hire an expert. But you can prepare, be ready, and look for the signs that an expert will get you where you want to go faster.

Plan to Hire Before You Think You're Ready

Let's face it. More often than not, we find ourselves scrambling for help when our to-do list is looking like a laundry list of forgotten tasks and our stress levels are charting new peaks. Does this sound uncomfortably familiar? If it does, let's raise a toast to our worldwide membership in the illustrious Procrastinators Club.

But why do we put off planning, especially when we know we need help? Here's a deeper dive into our chronic delay syndrome:

Mistaking the Deep End for the Shallow

It's human nature to underestimate the complexity of tasks that are outside our realm of expertise. It's the notorious Dunning-Kruger effect in action where our unconscious incompetence leads us to believe we can wrap up tasks quicker than we actually can.

Being Overly Sunny with Our Timelines

The sunniest of us tend to be overly optimistic about our timelines. This usually results in over-promising and under-delivering, leading to disappointment all around. A project delay not only dampens the team spirit but also productivity levels.

Time: An Elusive Commodity

In our race against time, we often find ourselves so swamped with work that we simply don't leave enough space for adequate planning. We are either running on overdrive trying to keep up with the daily grind or are too busy fighting fires to think about anything else.

The Hofstadter's Law Trap

If you've been around in the business world for a while, you'd know about the infamous Hofstadter's Law: It always takes longer than you expect, even when you take into account Hofstadter's Law. This axiom seems to hold a mirror to our planning fallacies, especially when we're embarking on something new.

When it comes to hiring experts, Hofstadter's Law rings particularly true.

The Art of Hiring: Adding More Arrows to Your Quiver

When we hire an expert, the goal is not just to get additional hands on deck. The true aim is to boost our ability to execute at a higher level while conserving our internal resources. It's like adding more arrows to our quiver so that we can hit our targets with greater accuracy and consistency.

So, the million-dollar question is… When should you start planning to hire an expert? To answer this, let's look at some guiding questions that can help assess if you might need to bring in an expert in the next quarter or half-year:

1. **Project Roadblocks.** Are there any projects in your company that are stuck, not initiated, or facing delays?

2. **Persistent Struggles.** Is your organization consistently struggling with specific aspects like finance, bookkeeping, taxes, hiring, training, communication, leads, sales, etc.?

3. **Operational Bottlenecks.** Do you find any critical bottlenecks or sticking points in your business operations?

4. **Underutilized Resources.** Are there any programs or applications that are not being used to their full potential, resulting in unnecessary costs?

5. **Lack of Expertise.** Is your company lacking in-house expertise on critical systems or programs?

6. **Growth Goals.** Are you planning substantial business growth in the near future, but don't have the necessary infrastructure or expertise to scale?

If you answered yes to any of the above, it's high time you considered hiring an expert.

The Timing Recipe: Mixing Intuition with Insight

Deciding to hire an expert is a bit like baking a cake. It's art mixed with science. You need to sift through your business needs, mix in some intuition, and bake it with insight.

Remember, the perfect time to hire an expert isn't a mythical moment in the future; it's when your business needs it. So be ready, be prepared, and be proactive. The early bird may catch the worm, but in the world of business the one who plans ahead is the one who enjoys a feast.

Evaluating If You're Ready to Hire

Wouldn't it be great if, like the dashboard of the car for oil changes, there was just an indicator that told us we needed to get help in our business? Sadly, that doesn't exist, and we are left to wrestle with our humanness when determining when to get expert help. Here are a few maneuvers we use to talk ourselves out of getting help, when the signs that we need assistance are already flashing.

I'm sure you've heard, or even whispered to yourself, these classic chants of the Help-Resistant:

- "I can't afford it."

- "I don't have time to train someone."

- "It's just easier to do it myself."

Sound familiar? These mantras echo through the corridors of businesses everywhere, and for a moment they may even seem true. It's crucial to shatter these illusions and face the reality: to thrive, we need support. We may be the leaders, but the best results come from a collective effort, from blending diverse skills and talents.

Let's dive into each Help-Resistant mantra and reflect upon its truth:

Affordability. When you say you can't afford help, is it really about the money? Or is it about seeing the value in investing in your business' future? Think about it. If you could hire an expert who could streamline your operations, wouldn't that free up your time to focus on growing your business?

Time. When you claim you don't have time to train someone, is it a genuine lack of time? Or could it be a reluctance to delegate, born out of the fear of losing control? If you delegate tasks, isn't it likely you'll eventually save time?

Simplicity. When you declare it's easier to do it yourself, is it really simpler? Or are you just familiar with the chaos? Remember, just because you *can* do something doesn't mean you *should*. Are there tasks someone else could perform more effectively, allowing you to use your unique skills where they are needed most?

It's important to recognize when we need assistance. The greatest accomplishments come from collaboration, teamwork and, yes, seeking help. Our minds may tempt us into believing we can do it all alone, but that's not how businesses flourish. We are intrinsically social beings, so it's natural and beneficial to build a network of experts to help us navigate our entrepreneurial journey.

Remember, seeking help isn't a sign of weakness. It's a testament to wisdom.

There are countless experienced individuals available who can provide valuable insights and guidance. The key is to be open to sharing the load and embracing a collaborative approach to success.

Deciding the Right Time and Embracing Help

Understanding when to hire and recognizing when you're prepared to collaborate with an expert isn't just about spotting a need. It's about being open to assistance, having the willingness to utilize the help, and the ability to integrate the skills and expertise brought in by the expert into your organization.

The Hiring Assessment: Your Business Health Check

Determining if you're ready to bring on new talent involves a thorough evaluation of various aspects of your business:

- **Growth Rate.** Assess how quickly your business is being asked to grow. Is it a manageable pace, or is the pressure escalating?

- **Team Skills.** Evaluate your current team's abilities. Do they possess the skills necessary for growth, or do they need support?

- **Team Workload.** Take a hard look at your team's workload. Is it sustainable, or are they overloaded?

- **New Initiatives.** If you're launching something new, consider whether some outside expertise could enhance success.

- **Team Development.** Are you aiming to build new skills within your existing team? Could external guidance accelerate this?

- **Available Resources.** Consider what resources you have to handle growth, improvement, or an increased workload.

- **Accountability.** Monitor the progress being made on tasks. Are your projects moving forward at a satisfactory pace?

Making It Quantifiable: The Scorecard Approach

To make this assessment tangible, consider creating a score-card. Rate each area on a scale of 1 to 5, where 1 indicates complete control and 5 represents a challenging situation.

Also, consider adding a second score for each area that signifies the urgency or difficulty of that aspect. If your combined score reaches 15 or higher, you likely need expert assistance.

Increasing Readiness Through Inquiry

Interestingly, the simple act of questioning your readiness enhances your preparedness to bring in an expert. Understanding your expectations, desired outcomes, and the changes you want to see prepares you better for hiring and benefiting from external expertise.

To aid this process, here are some additional questions to contemplate:

- Which areas or team members require consistent attention?

- Where is your business failing to meet your success metrics?

- What parts of your operations are causing considerable stress or are consistently neglected?

- Are there aspects of your business operations that remain unclear or undefined?

- Where is your business experiencing high turnover or incurring excessive costs?

By examining these areas, you'll be better equipped to decide when and where expert assistance can be most beneficial. The goal is not just to hire help, but to align it with your business needs effectively, to drive growth and success.

Case Study: Timing Matters (a Lot)

The Situation

In the world of business, no one ever said that navigating the sea of opportunity was smooth sailing. Let's take a journey with an agency that we've consulted with. They've carved out a niche for themselves, creating stunning presentation designs for large multinational corporations—a service that you'd think would be in constant demand.

However, there's a curious hiccup that they keep encountering. More often than not, the first project they propose to a new client doesn't take off. The proposal gets submitted, the discussions happen, but then the deal peters out. Now, this might seem strange to an outside observer. What could be going wrong?

When we delved deeper, we found that the clients saw value in the service. The agency's designs were striking, and they offered a thorough and professional approach. The real issue was a race against time. The prospective clients, keen to make their mark with powerful presentations, would reach out a mere two to three weeks before the big event - it just wasn't enough time for this agency to deliver.

The Plan

Now, let's consider the nature of these presentations. They are not just any old slide shows meant for a low-key internal meeting. These are high-visibility events that have the potential to shape careers and influence business strategies. We're talking about executive pitches or investor relations presentations. In such high-stakes situations, would you trust a new agency with your slides just three weeks out? Probably not. The risk would be too high.

This revelation struck the agency owner. The potential clients were trapped in a time crunch, and they were unwilling to entrust an untested agency with such a crucial task at the eleventh hour. He realized he had to change his approach to help his clients and his business.

In understanding this problem, the agency owner saw an opportunity to transform this challenge into a strength. He noticed that many clients were not entirely satisfied with their current agency. They complained about the lack of creativity, the humdrum designs and the repetitive concepts, but they were resigned to sticking with them due to time constraints.

Getting to Work

This is where the agency owner introduced a groundbreaking concept: early engagement. He started encouraging prospective clients to begin their conversations with his agency long before the actual presentation was due. This strategy would allow both parties sufficient time to understand each other's needs and expectations.

Initiating the conversation many months in advance can seem like a radical departure from traditional practices. However, it is this forward-thinking approach that brings a host of benefits.

Firstly, there's no rush to make a decision. The client can take their time to familiarize themselves with the agency's style and techniques. Secondly, the agency has the opportunity to fully understand the client's requirements and the presentation's objectives.

All this preparation serves to build a solid foundation of trust and understanding. From this firm base, both parties can work together to create a presentation that meets the client's needs and aligns with the agency's capabilities.

The Result

To manage this process, the agency recommended implementing a forward-thinking strategy. This involved having a dedicated team member, either from within the company or externally, looking at upcoming projects 6 to 12 months in advance. They would be responsible for setting recommended kickoff dates for projects to ensure their clients extracted maximum value from the agency's services.

Here's an uncomfortable truth: deadline crunches and 'out-of-timeness' are not just stressful; they are self-perpetuating. They lock businesses into a vicious cycle of panic and rush, making each project feel like a race against time. It's an all-too-familiar sensation—that sinking feeling in the pit of your stomach, the constricted breathing as deadlines loom.

Breaking free from this stressful cycle requires a deliberate, conscious effort. It means setting aside time to plan, strategize, communicate with external resources, and make decisions about hiring experts. It involves challenging the status quo and being comfortable with doing things differently.

Lessons Learned

The payoff is huge. Imagine a work life without constant panic, without the nagging feeling of always being a step behind. Imagine having a plan in place and the confidence that you have the capacity to handle whatever comes your way. That's the reward you reap when you hire an expert.

This case study is a testament to that. By adjusting their approach, the agency owner was able to break the cycle of panic and last-minute rush, thereby empowering clients to plan better and create presentations that truly delivered value. The result was a win-win situation: happy clients and a thriving agency.

The overarching lesson is clear: Early engagement is key to successfully hiring an expert and getting the best out of their services. So start early, plan strategically, and embrace the rewarding experience of working with experts.

Chapter Three

When NOT to Hire an Expert

So far, we've traversed the many avenues where hiring an expert can work wonders for your business. We've explored how hiring experts can catalyze growth, empower your team, and inject a fresh perspective into your operations. But let's hit the pause button for a moment. What about the times when hiring an expert might not be the best move?

Indeed, even the most experienced experts are not superheroes or wizards. They don't possess a magic wand that can resolve all challenges, and they certainly don't come with an 'all-problems-solved' guarantee. They have specific areas of expertise, and their skills are fine-tuned to address certain problems, not all.

So, while an expert can often be a game-changer, there are scenarios where seeking their assistance might not be the optimal solution. Sometimes, the solution lies within your team's capabilities, or perhaps the issue is something that requires a different approach entirely.

In this chapter, we'll explore those situations where it's best to hold off on hiring an expert. It's about understanding that every problem doesn't warrant an external expert solution and identifying those times when you can leverage the talent that already exists within your organization, or when a different strategy might be the key to unlocking success.

Here are the reasons NOT to hire an expert:

To Create an Illusion of Improvement

Deciding to hire an expert often comes from a well-intentioned place. Your company identifies a task it "should" be doing and brings in an expert to fast-track the process, effectively leapfrogging the initial learning curve and associated growing pains. At face value this can look like a strategic move, an investment in growth.

But here's the catch: this approach frequently culminates in a project's completion without any lasting benefit to the company. You find yourself at the finish line, but it's a hollow victory. The results are ephemeral and the positive change elusive.

This lack of retained value doesn't occur because the expert was ill-equipped or didn't know their craft. Quite the contrary, they might be masters in their field. The hiccup, surprisingly, often originates from the company's own resistance. The business owner, the team, or the entire department might not be ready or willing to truly embrace the change.

My first encounter with this phenomenon came when a company I worked for decided to become ISO 9001-certified. This certification—a respected symbol of manufacturing quality management—was our designated finish line.

We hired an expert, diligent and experienced, who guided us through the demanding certification process. We jumped through hoops, tackled hurdles, and finally achieved what we set out to do. We became ISO 9001-certified.

Yet, once the dust had settled and the applause subsided, we realized something. Apart from the shiny certificate adorning our office wall, nothing had changed. Our daily operations remained unchanged, our work methodologies were untouched. No substantial improvement had been realized.

The only difference was that we were now a certified entity, but our ground reality was unaltered. We hadn't moved the needle forward for growth, improvement, or capacity. We had simply checked off a box that we thought we 'should', without understanding if it was something that we truly needed.

Unpacking the 'Should': Decoding the Misalignment

The ISO experience, while initially a disappointment, turned out to be an invaluable lesson. We realized that the failure wasn't because of a lack of effort or expertise. Instead, it was due to a fundamental misalignment of our goals.

We pursued the certification because we believed we 'should', not because we identified a specific need that the certification would address. We failed to ask ourselves how this change would enhance our growth or improve our capacity. The outcome was a disconnect between the task, the team, and the expected result.

An essential factor we overlooked was the willingness of our team to embrace change. Just bringing in an expert and expecting transformation can lead to resistance, especially if the team does not understand or appreciate the need for change.

When a change is imposed or feels forced, it's often met with resistance. Genuine change is not just about implementing new systems or achieving certifications. It's about nurturing a mindset that welcomes evolution, encourages learning, and fosters improvement.

Key Takeaway: Aligning Change with Need

Before deciding to hire an expert, ask yourself: "Are we doing this because we 'should', or are we doing this because it aligns with our business needs and goals?" Remember, the drive for change should come from a genuine business need, not just a perceived obligation.

Hiring an expert is a powerful tool, but it's not a magic bullet. It should be a strategic move, motivated by the specific needs of your business and embraced by your team. The decision to hire an expert should be part of a bigger picture of growth, improvement and capacity-building, not a superficial addition of a certificate or an imposed change.

The Paradox of Non-Participation

Hiring an expert, especially in a 'done-for-you' scenario, may sound like an alluring prospect. You get a skilled professional, a person with niche expertise, who takes on the entire project and frees you from all the nitty-gritty details. They're at the helm, managing the tactical execution, crafting strategic plans, extracting and analyzing information. A neat package of convenience and expertise, right? Not quite. There's an essential component of the expert-client dynamic that often gets overlooked—your active participation.

Oddly enough, the most challenging task for an expert is not the hands-on execution or the extensive planning. It's not about coaxing information out of the client or managing unexpected hurdles. The real Herculean task is inciting the requisite mindset change in you, the client.

That's right. The crux of an expert's work, the part that can make or break the success of a project, is shifting your mindset from where you are today to where you want to be. And this isn't something that can be done without your active participation.

Change: More Than Just a Physical Transformation

Any significant change, be it personal or professional, is more than just a physical transformation. It's not merely about updating systems or implementing new strategies. True change requires an alteration in thought processes, a shift in the way you perceive and approach things.

An expert can provide the tools, the roadmap, and even walk alongside you, but the actual journey, the internal transformation, has to come from within you. This involves being open to new perspectives, embracing novel methods, and sometimes unlearning old habits.

If you're resistant to this mindset change, if you're unwilling to participate in this transformation process, hiring an expert might end up being less beneficial than you'd hoped. An expert can lay out the best strategies, but unless you are ready to actively engage, understand, and incorporate these changes the path to your desired destination can become murky.

The importance of a mindset change cannot be overstated. Your participation is the fuel propelling this change. As the driving force behind your business, when your mindset shifts your business shifts.

Before you decide to hire an expert, take a moment to reflect. Are you ready to actively participate, not just in the tangible aspects but in the internal, mindset-altering part of the journey? If not, you might want to reassess.

Remember, even in a 'done-for-you' scenario, you're not just a spectator. You're a key player. Your engagement, your willingness to adapt, and your readiness to embrace new thought processes are pivotal to the project's success.

In the end, hiring an expert is a partnership, a dance where both parties are essential for the performance to be a success. It's not just about having someone do the work for you; it's about growing and evolving together to reach your ultimate goals. And that, my friend, requires your participation.

Only You Can Change Your Core Beliefs

When it comes to hiring experts, there's a crucial aspect to remember: No expert, regardless of their experience, skills, or credentials, can change your core beliefs for you. They might be masters in their respective fields, proficient at problem-solving and strategy crafting. Yet they remain powerless against the fortress of your deep-seated beliefs.

The finest experts out there have honed an additional set of skills beyond their field of expertise. These skills allow them to guide you gently yet effectively through transitional periods, serving as a lighthouse as you navigate through change. However, let's remember this process necessitates your and your organization's willingness to undertake the emotional heavy lifting involved in modifying your beliefs and the behaviors stemming from them.

When we talk about emotional heavy lifting we refer to the intense, often challenging process of altering your deep-rooted beliefs and the behaviors they induce. This is no small feat. It demands introspection, vulnerability, and courage. It involves peeling back layers of long-held beliefs, questioning their validity, and molding them anew.

Experts can serve as guides in this process, providing you with tools and techniques to facilitate change. Yet the actual work, the pushing against ingrained patterns and embracing new perspectives, falls on your shoulders.

Honest Reflection: A Prerequisite to Change

Before taking the leap to hire an expert, pause for some candid self-reflection. Are you genuinely willing to be an active participant in the process of change? Are you prepared to dig deep, to face and alter ingrained beliefs? This journey goes beyond surface-level change; it delves into the depths of who you are and how you operate.

This process may very well demand that you undertake some deeper work, venturing into the inner recesses of your being to face and transform the beliefs nestled there. It's not a path for the faint-hearted. It calls for courage, resilience, and openness.

However, be assured that this journey, though challenging, is also immensely rewarding. It can lead to profound transformation and growth, not just on a personal level but also for your organization. It creates a ripple effect, impacting your perspectives, your decisions and, ultimately, your business's overall trajectory.

Don't hire an expert if your organization isn't ready to change. You need to already be willing to shoulder the emotional load and to face and transform deeply-entrenched beliefs. Remember, an expert is a guide, not a governor of change. The ultimate power for transformation lies within you.

You Won't Let Them Do Their Job

It's surprisingly common for organizations to hire experts and then unwittingly become their own roadblocks by not permitting the experts to fully do their job. It might seem absurd—why hire an expert if you're not ready to loosen the reins? Yet it happens more often than you might imagine.

Of course, most of us believe that you'd let an expert do their job. After all, you hired them for their expertise and are going to pay them. But before you bring someone onboard, take a moment to reflect on your previous engagements with experts. Did they pan out as expected? Were the experts given enough room to exercise their skills and bring about positive changes? Or were they hindered, consciously or not, by the organization's reluctance to let go of the wheel?

Working effectively with experts requires an openness to change. Whether it's adopting a new technology, altering a business strategy or overhauling an organizational structure, a degree of flexibility is crucial. If change is seen as a threat rather than an opportunity, the organization will likely resist the expert's suggestions and strategies, resulting in a lack of long-term value from the expert's efforts.

Herein lies the paradox: while an expert is hired to instigate change, the organization must be open to change for the expert's efforts to bear fruit. If the organization is steadfast in its old ways, resistant to change and inflexible, it's like trying to drive a car with the brakes on—it just won't move.

Resistance to change can be a significant barrier to your organization's success. It impedes progress, stifles innovation, and hinders an expert's ability to do their job effectively. If your organization has a history of resisting change, it may be wise to address this issue before bringing another expert on board.

Change Agents: An Expert for Change

There are experts who specialize in facilitating change within organizations, paving the way for other experts to do their job effectively. These change agents can help create a culture that embraces change, setting the stage for future collaborations with experts.

But it all starts with awareness. Recognize if resistance to change is a hurdle your organization needs to overcome. If it is, consider bringing in an expert who can help your organization foster an environment of adaptability and growth.

You Need a Rescue Squad

The allure of a quick rescue is a powerful thing, especially in the midst of a crisis. Experts are often seen as the knight in shining armor, swooping in to save the day. And sometimes they can indeed deliver that swift, satisfying resolution you're desperately seeking. But most of the time, hiring an expert isn't about executing a rapid rescue mission; it's about facilitating lasting change and cultivating long-term success.

So what happens when your organization is in a bind and you're convinced that you need a rescue squad? That's when you need to take a step back and evaluate your expectations.

Evaluating Urgency and Intent

Is the urgency you're feeling real, or is it a perceived pressure? What's the true purpose of the project or task at hand? What does a successful outcome look like? In many instances, once you slow down and examine the core reasons behind a project and what needs to occur to achieve success you'll realize that the urgency is more imagined than real. No emergency rescue squad is required; what's needed instead is a reset of expectations.

The Hidden Costs of External Triage

Calling in outside help to triage issues can be resource-intensive. Not only does it involve financial costs, but it also demands time and effort to bring the experts on board and familiarize them with your organization's processes and nuances. On the other hand, internal triage, though challenging, encourages your team to develop problem-solving capabilities, increasing your organization's resilience over time.

The Pitfalls of a Quick-Fix Mentality

Relying too heavily on external 'fixers' doesn't contribute to your organization's growth, improvement, or true capacity building. In fact, this approach might lead your organization into a trap of perpetual victimhood, always needing outside help and never developing internal problem-solving skills. This is why continuous dependence on 'rescuers' is listed as a reason not to hire an expert.

Revisiting the Purpose of Hiring Experts

The essence of bringing in outside help is to foster growth, drive improvement, and enhance capacity. If your reasons for considering external help don't align with these categories, you might need to rethink your decision.

Let's be clear: Experts can undoubtedly be of immense help in emergencies, but their real value lies in their ability to bring about long-term, sustainable changes. Therefore, before you send out a distress signal, pause, assess your situation, and understand what you truly need: a quick fix or sustainable change.

The Bottom Line: Cultivate, Don't Just Rescue

Ultimately, the idea behind hiring an expert is not to patch a leak temporarily but to enhance your ship's overall seaworthiness. Continually rescuing without improving won't lead to the growth and success you desire. By understanding this, you can better decide when to hire experts and how to make the most out of their expertise.

Uncertainty in Scope and Success: A Red Flag

There's an old saying: "If you don't know where you're going, any road will get you there." This applies profoundly when it comes to hiring an expert. If your project's scope of work or measure of success is hazy, it's like embarking on a journey without a clear destination. It's neither fair to the expert you're considering to hire nor beneficial to your organization.

The Importance of Clarity

Clarity on project scope and success metrics forms the bedrock of effective collaboration with an expert. It defines the expert's boundaries and sets clear expectations on what they're supposed to deliver. Without this clarity you're setting the stage for potential misunderstandings, disappointment, and even conflict down the line.

Evaluating Your Readiness to Hire

If you're grappling with an unclear scope or success metrics, it might be worthwhile revisiting the earlier section, "Evaluating if You Are Ready To Hire." There, you'll find valuable insights on determining when it's time to hire. It'll help you assess your preparedness to bring on an expert, ensuring you have all the necessary pieces in place before you take that significant step.

Proceed with Confidence

Ultimately, clarity fosters trust and confidence. Both are crucial for a successful partnership with an expert. It allows the expert to deliver their best work and your organization to leverage their expertise effectively. So before bringing in an expert, ensure you have crystal-clear answers to two key questions: What needs to be done? And how will we know we've succeeded?

Seeking Affirmation, Not Expertise

"Echo chamber." It's a term we often hear in the world of social media, but it's a concept that, unfortunately, can seep into our professional lives, too. If you're considering hiring an expert simply to have them reaffirm your ideas, beliefs, or strategies, you might be falling into this trap. It's critical to remember that if you're merely seeking validation, acceptance, or permission, what you're after isn't an expert—it's an echo.

Chasing Agreement Over Innovation

Experts are individuals who possess a deep understanding of a specific field, who can analyze situations with a keen eye and offer unique insights and novel solutions. They are not 'yes' men or women, nodding in approval at every suggestion. By seeking a professional who will only echo your thoughts, you're undercutting the true value of their expertise. You're stifling innovation, suppressing new ideas, and potentially barricading the path to meaningful growth.

Expertise Means Embracing Challenge

When we bring on an expert, we're not just hiring their knowledge—we're also employing their capacity to challenge us. They'll push our boundaries, question our assumptions, and sometimes outright disagree with us. This process, while sometimes uncomfortable, is where the magic of growth happens. It's through this intellectual tug-of-war that fresh perspectives emerge and innovative solutions are born.

Uncover Your True Needs

So, if you find yourself angling for the answers you want to hear, it might be time for a bit of introspection. It could be an indication that what you really need isn't an expert's input but perhaps self-validation, the confidence to trust your instincts, or the courage to take a new leap. In the end, an expert's job is not to tell you what you want to hear but what you need to hear, for the betterment of your organization. And that's the real value of their expertise.

There's a Time & Place for Everything, Including Experts

In our world of quick fixes and jumping on the fastest train to success, the message of not hiring an expert might feel a bit counterintuitive. Yet, knowing when not to hire an expert is as crucial as knowing when to do so. It's about understanding your project, your team, and at the core, your own strengths and weaknesses.

While experts can be the turbo boosters of your project or business needs, it's essential to recognize that there are times when it's better to hold back, use your own team's capabilities, slow the pace or use a different strategy.

The Illusion of Progress, the Paradox of Non-Participation, and the depth of your own Core Beliefs bring our attention to the times when an expert isn't the solution you need. Recognizing when You Won't Let Them Do Their Job or when you're just after affirmation, not expertise, can save you a lot of wasted effort and resources too.

As you are learning, an expert isn't a magician who can make every problem disappear. They're humans like us, specialized in their field. So the next time you're wrestling with a problem, use what you are learning here to take a beat and assess if you need an expert or if you just need a different approach.

Chapter Four
Ways to Work
with an Expert

The whole point of engaging with an expert is to grow, improve, or add capacity.

As we embark on the last chapter of Part 1: Base Camp, let's dive deeper into the heart of the matter: the core reasons for engaging with an expert. It's easy to generalize the rationale as the need for expertise, yet it's much more nuanced than that. There are essentially three fundamental pillars that often drive the decision to engage with an expert—to grow, to improve, or to add capacity.

Just as a gardener carefully nurtures a seedling, enabling it to flourish, engaging with an expert can significantly contribute to your business' growth. This growth might take the form of scaling your operations, expanding your market reach, or increasing your revenue. However, it's not just about numerical growth; it can also entail developing a more mature business approach, enhancing your processes, or building a more robust brand.

Improvement is another significant catalyst behind the decision to collaborate with an expert. Whether it's enhancing the efficiency of your workflow, improving the quality of your product or service or fostering a more positive workplace culture, expert assistance can catalyze remarkable improvements. These improvements, while they may seem incremental at first, can compound over time to yield substantial benefits.

Then we have capacity—perhaps the most tangible of the three pillars. There's only so much a single individual or team can handle, and there are times when the demands of the business exceed this threshold. An expert can come in to add capacity, effectively serving as a force multiplier, enabling your organization to tackle more tasks, take on larger projects, or simply alleviate the strain on your existing resources.

Navigating the nuances of these pillars and understanding which one (or more) is relevant for you is crucial to determine the type of expert you need. You might even find it beneficial to consult an expert to help answer this very question. It's here where the concept of free consultations can shine, turning an exploratory conversation into a vital strategic decision-making tool.

However, to extract the most value from such a consultation, you need to come prepared. Entering a consultation without a clear agenda can easily make the discussion veer off-course, turning it into a sales pitch. To avoid this, strive to articulate your problem or at least the symptoms you're seeking to address. Doing so equips the expert with the necessary context to help connect the dots for you and propose a potential solution.

Before we delve into the exact strategy to approach such consultations, it's crucial to understand the breadth of possibilities. The ways you can engage with an expert are nearly as diverse as the number of stars in the sky. From one-off projects and long-term partnerships to advisory roles and part-time engagements, the range is vast. As we navigate this final chapter of Part 1, we'll explore these diverse modes of engagement, equipping you with the knowledge to make the best decision for your unique needs.

Ways to Work with an Expert

The digital age we find ourselves in today has ushered in a new era of unprecedented accessibility. We're no longer limited by physical boundaries or by the constraints of our immediate networks. Thanks to the internet, there's a veritable wealth of expertise at our fingertips—a global smorgasbord of specialists across countless fields and industries.

Yes, the spectrum of expertise available for hire today is almost comically vast. Just to illustrate the point, have you ever heard of professional bridesmaids? That's right, in this wide array of specialized professions you can even find someone who has honed their skill at being a bridesmaid to a fine art and can attend your wedding, standing by your side, adding their pro-

fessional finesse to your special day. Who could have anticipated such an incredibly niche role becoming a professional
service? Yet here we are!

This anecdote demonstrates that today's landscape of expertise
is not only varied, but practically limitless. And equally varied
are the ways in which you can engage with these experts. The
modes of engagement with an expert can span from monthly
coaching sessions to full-scale outsourcing, to absorbing
knowledge through courses and books (like you're doing right
now!). There's no single, universal format for how you should
work with an expert. Instead, there exists a diverse array of possibilities, enabling you to find a mode of engagement that best
suits your unique needs.

Consultants

Consulting is often the first form of expert engagement that
comes to mind. But we're not talking about the archetypal, jar-
gon-spewing consultants of old. Instead, we're referring to industry experts who, like seasoned detectives, can scrutinize
your business, identify inefficiencies and bottlenecks, and suggest targeted improvements. These consultants may not be the
ones implementing the changes, but the insights they provide
can be immensely valuable.

In-House Experts

Yet for those who seek a more hands-on approach or need to
expand their business's operational capacity, an in-house expert
could be the answer. This is like bringing an experienced

climber on board, someone who doesn't just show you the ropes but helps you scale the mountain as well. With an expert as part of your team, they can champion projects, mentor your staff, and play a pivotal role in driving your business towards its goals. Services such as Fractional C-suite roles, like CFO or CMO, enable you to harness this expertise and leadership without incurring the cost of a full-time salary or making long-term commitments.

Freelancers

However, the idea of bringing an expert in-house might seem daunting, both in terms of commitment and resources. Here's where freelancers come into play. These are the multi-tool Swiss Army knives of the business world—adaptable, versatile, and ready for action whenever you need them. Freelancers can handle specific projects, fill gaps in your workforce or offer fresh perspectives, all without requiring permanent resources from your end.

Agencies

If managing additional people even on a freelance basis still seems too much, consider outsourcing to an agency. These specialist organizations, focusing on areas like IT, marketing, accounting, or systems, offer a comprehensive solution. By partnering with an agency you gain access to an entire team of experts, minus the intricacies of managing individuals. Furthermore, these agencies usually come with established processes and systems, meaning even less groundwork for you.

Choose Your Own Engagement

Honestly, the variations in types of engagement are so numerous, it's nearly impossible to list them all. At our agency, we often find that the most successful collaborations with clients involve a mix of consulting, strategizing, planning, implementation, and training.

So remember, there are countless ways to work with experts. If you ever find yourself thinking, "I can't find someone who can XYZ," consider this a challenge to broaden your perspective and explore different modes of engagement. There's an entire world of expertise out there, waiting to be harnessed in ways you may have not even considered before.

The vast landscape of expertise out there today includes not only people you can hire but also an extensive repertoire of resources available to you. Sometimes, the expert you need may not even be a person. It could be a book that provides a deep dive into your problem area, a well-structured program, or an enlightening online course. In the ever-evolving digital age, there's also a burgeoning array of apps specifically designed to deliver expertise at your fingertips.

Here are some types of experts who can help you and questions you can ask yourself to recognize which type of expert help is best for you.

Common Business Experts:

- Consultant (of any & all types, business, financial, engineering, software, marketing, etc.)

- Accountant

- Bookkeeper

- Lawyer

- Coach (business, life, speaking, skincare, etc.)

- Designer

- Developer

- Marketer

- Assistant

Less Common Business Experts:

- Maternity Leave Coaches

- Work Sitter

- House Cleaner

- Personal Chef

- Online System Setup Consultant/Agency

- Mechanic

- Meal Prep/Delivery Service

- Tax Strategist

Hiring the Right Expert for the Job

Navigating the labyrinth of hiring an expert can often be a challenging task, especially if we're not entirely sure what we're looking for. The inability to articulate our needs might stem from a lack of knowledge about the problem we're trying to solve. Or conversely, it might be the result of the "Curse of Knowledge"—the cognitive bias where we are so entrenched in a problem or so intimately familiar with a topic that we can't see the forest for the trees. In either case, a gap in clarity or perspective can leave us floundering, unsure of who to enlist to help solve our problem.

So how do you differentiate between whether you need an analytics expert, an ecommerce specialist, a consultant, a coach, or even a book or an app? Where does one even begin the journey to find the correct expert? The myriad choices available to us can often be overwhelming, leaving us feeling like a sailor lost at sea without a compass.

Over the years, I've seen countless instances where potential clients approach us with a predefined notion of what they need. A common scenario is a business owner seeking a web designer with the aim of extracting more value from their website through a redesign. Yet upon dissecting their challenges and delving into their requirements, it often surfaces that what they need isn't a web designer at all. Their actual need might lie in crafting a more robust sales strategy, or perhaps in developing a method to capture leads more effectively, or even in creating an email strategy. The problem they need solving frequently has little to do with their initial presumption.

This is precisely why getting a firm handle on the problem you're trying to solve is a pivotal first step in identifying the expert you genuinely need. It's like finding the North Star—a reference point to orient yourself and direct your journey towards the right expertise.

To select the best-fit expert and identify the optimal mode of engagement, you first need to roll up your sleeves and do the groundwork. This means diving deep into your problem, scrutinizing it from every angle, and defining what your desired outcome looks like. You must envisage the end result of a successful engagement. What does success look like for you?

And remember, there's no shame in seeking help to define the problem you're trying to solve. Experts exist for a reason—their depth of knowledge, experience, and unique perspectives can often shine a light on the path you need to take. Even if you start the journey with a foggy view of the road ahead, the right expert can provide the clarity you need and guide you towards a solution.

This process isn't always straightforward or easy. It requires patience, open-mindedness, and a willingness to confront potentially unfamiliar areas. But the end result—finding an expert who can provide not just a solution, but the right solution— makes it all worthwhile. The journey of identifying the right expert might be challenging, but it's an indispensable part of the path to problem-solving and growth.

Get Clear About Your Core Problem Before You Hire

In the world of problem-solving and seeking expert help, one might be tempted to race towards the finish line, jump straight to a solution, and breathe a sigh of relief. However, leaping headfirst into a solution without truly understanding the nature of the problem is like treating the symptom while ignoring the disease. The chances are that this approach will result in short-term relief at best, and the issue is likely to recur, often with more significant ramifications.

Instead of this rush towards remedy, investing time in understanding your problem's intricacies is an incredibly worthwhile endeavor. Evaluating your resources, and constraints such as time, financial considerations, your team's capacity and the effort you can put in will equip you with a better understanding. This clarity provides you with the power to make an informed decision on how to engage with the expertise you require.

To aid in this process, there are a few critical questions to ponder. A self-interrogation of sorts to get to the crux of your needs:

1. **What is my main problem?** Here, it's crucial to dig deep, peeling layer after layer of the issue, like peeling

an onion, until you strike the core. To aid in this process, continuously ask yourself, "And then what?" Probing your assumptions and challenging your conclusions by asking, "Is that actually true?" can be immensely helpful. Like the clients who approached me thinking they needed a web designer, your actual problem might be a layer or two deeper than just the symptoms you're experiencing.

2. **How quickly do I want or need to achieve results?** Time is a critical factor in problem-solving. Understanding your timeline can dictate the type of expert you need. Do you need a quick fix, or are you looking for a long-term solution? Knowing your desired timeline can help guide you to the right expert or solution.

3. **Who is involved already?** Understanding who is already part of the solution can greatly influence the type of expert you need. Do you already have a team in place that needs direction, or are you starting from scratch?

4. **What resources do I have to spend?** Resources can be multifaceted. Is there a budget allocated for this purpose? Do you have team members available to work on this issue? Your available resources include not only money but also manpower and time. A clear understanding of what's at your disposal will guide you to the most feasible solution.

By answering these questions, you develop a more comprehensive understanding of your problem and what it will take to solve it. This process also provides a roadmap for the kind of expert you need to hire. An expert is like a guide in a foreign land. In order to direct you to your destination, they must first understand where you are and what resources you have for the journey. The clearer your understanding of your problem and the resources at your disposal, the better your expert can lead you to the solution. It's about setting up a mutual understanding between you and your expert, allowing for a more effective and efficient problem-solving process.

Finding the Right Solution

Okay, so you've reached a clear understanding of your problem and the resources available to tackle it. Now you arrive at the next critical juncture: finding the right solution. The task now is to dive into the world of expertise related to your issue and identify your best match. However, this isn't your permission slip to sprint off to Google and commence an impromptu research marathon.

Let's be frank. If the solution to your problem were readily accessible through a quick Google search, you probably wouldn't be grappling with the issue in the first place. As you might already be aware, there's an entire industry of experts diligently decoding search terms to link your problem with an answer on the internet. However, without a clear idea of what to search for, the chances of hitting the bullseye are rather slim.

Instead, consider your research as a series of conversations. Reach out to people within your network who you trust and who might have encountered a similar problem. Their experience and insights into how they resolved their issues can be incredibly valuable. We often underestimate the wealth of knowledge and wisdom that resides within our own circles.

Having gathered some initial insight, you might identify a few experts who seem well-suited to your needs. Take the next step by booking consultations with them. The purpose of these discussions is not just to get a quote or a sales pitch, but to genuinely understand how they operate, the services they provide and, most importantly, how they might address your unique situation.

Here's an insider tip: Don't feel limited by the standard offerings of the expert you're interested in. If their services don't precisely align with your preferred way of working, it's perfectly fine to ask for alternatives. Experts are often flexible and open to crafting bespoke engagement plans. For instance, recently, several of my clients approached me about establishing ongoing monthly consulting sessions. This wasn't a standard service we provided, but upon discussing their needs we successfully set up a series of regular monthly appointments. The key takeaway is this: Don't hesitate to voice your needs and preferences. Experts are generally receptive to engagement styles that differ from their standard offerings.

Conclusion

Let's take a moment to recap what we've covered. We've looked at the various ways you can work with an expert, including hiring, consultancy, freelancing, and more. We've explored critical self-reflective questions that help you identify the type of expert that might be best suited to address your problem. We've highlighted the importance of thorough research, primarily through conversations with trusted individuals in your network.

But now comes the million-dollar question: Are you actually ready to hire an expert? The answer to this question isn't always as straightforward as it may seem. Hiring an expert is a significant decision, often involving considerable time, effort, and financial commitment. Therefore, it's crucial to ensure that you're truly ready to embark on this journey. In the next chapter we'll delve deeper into this topic to help you make an informed decision, setting you on a successful path to problem-resolution.

We've navigated some tricky terrain, explored some common misconceptions, and laid a solid groundwork for how to approach the decision-making process of hiring an expert. By sharing tales from our work with various agencies and clients, we've offered a glimpse into the complexities and pitfalls that often accompany the journey of seeking external expertise.

In the many narratives we've encountered, a common thread appears to bind the stories of missteps and mishaps: that the majority stem from either unvoiced expectations or unrealistic assumptions about what an expert can or should do.

The scenarios where the engagement with an expert leads to frustration, failure, or generally undesirable outcomes often have their roots in these misconceptions. Like any ill-fated adventure, embarking on a quest to find expert help without the right preparation can lead you astray, into the dark forest of disappointment and wasted resources.

This doesn't have to be your story. We've seen that the alternative narrative, the one where the journey to hiring an expert ends in success, typically begins with a critical ingredient: thoughtful reflection. Taking the time for introspection, to deeply understand what you need help with, and to identify if you're unknowingly walking into any of the common traps associated with hiring an expert can significantly tilt the odds of success in your favor. It's akin to taking a flashlight with you as you venture into the forest, illuminating your path and helping you avoid the pitfalls that lie hidden in the undergrowth.

This thoughtful reflection, this flashlight, is what equips you to hire the right kind of expert; one who will not just fulfill a role but truly partner with you to realize your goals. It raises your chances of a successful collaboration exponentially, turning what could have been a daunting venture into a fruitful partnership.

We explored the various methods of engaging with experts, from consultancy and in-house hires to freelancing and outsourcing. We unraveled the importance of clearly identifying your core problem before bringing in an expert, and how you could find the most suitable solution within the vast sea of expertise available. This process of careful reflection and methodical decision-making is your torch, equipping you to hire the right kind of expert—one who will not merely fill a role but genuinely partner with you to achieve your objectives.

And now, as we venture into Part 2: Engagement, we're going to wade deeper into the how-tos of hiring the right experts. Now that we've armed ourselves with the knowledge of when to hire and when not to hire, it's time to turn our focus towards the practical aspects of identifying, selecting, and working with the right experts. The next part of our journey will equip you with the tools and strategies you need to effectively engage with experts, ensuring that you gain the maximum value from these collaborations.

Remember, hiring an expert is more than just filling a role. It's about creating a partnership that fosters growth, drives improvement, and enhances your capacity. And that's precisely what we'll explore in Part 2: The Climb. So keep your flashlight handy, and let's embark on the next leg of our journey. Your path to engaging effectively with experts starts here.

PART II
The Climb

Welcome to Part Two of our transformative journey, fairly obviously titled 'The Climb'. Here is where we venture into the thrilling (or terrifying) ascent, unraveling the mystery of expert engagement, and guiding you through the sometimes treacherous terrain of hiring the right expert, preparing your organization for expert engagement, and addressing any potential detours along the path.

The climb might appear daunting initially, but every journey begins with a single step, and even when things don't go to plan, there's always another way to your goal. This segment aims to arm you with the necessary insights and expertise to make that first step, and those that follow, with confidence and clarity.

Bear in mind, the climb we're embarking on isn't simply about ascending - it's about appreciating the journey, learning from each turn, and applying acquired wisdom to enrich not just the specific project at hand, but your overall strategic approach. Read on to reveal the mysteries of expert engagement, illumination for the path, and preparing for the high-altitude adventure of establishing and nurturing successful expert relationships.

Through real-world case studies, you'll see these principles in action, exploring how other business owners have navigated potential pitfalls and got back on the path.

Detours, although unexpected, are part of any journey. A few likely scenarios that might cause your venture to veer off-course are outlined as well as ways to handle these situations to maintain momentum and stay on the path to success.

Chapter Five
Which Expert to Hire?

Ah, decisions. They are our constant companions, aren't they? And yet making them can be as confounding as solving a Rubik's Cube while blindfolded. Take for instance my son's go-to decision-making method: "eenie meenie minee mo." Cute, right? A quintessential childhood strategy that serves him well when he's picking between popsicle flavors or deciding which t-shirt to wear. However, when it comes to the higher stakes arena of your business, the "eenie meenie minee mo" approach may not be the wisest course of action, particularly when you're faced with the all-important decision of which expert to hire.

Now, don't get me wrong. Choosing an expert to bring into your business is not like picking the right answer on a multiple-choice test. Oh, how I wish it was that straightforward! No, this is more akin to navigating a maze with numerous possible paths, each leading to a different kind of expert. The journey through this maze is fraught with challenges and questions. Can you trust this expert? Do you need a web designer or a web developer? Maybe a marketing director? Or perhaps a systems optimization agency like ours? It's like standing at a crossroads with a multitude of signposts all pointing in different directions.

And let's not even get started on the buzzwords and jargon that experts love to throw around! It's enough to make your head spin faster than a carousel. Let me tell you a little secret, though. The industry titles? They're just fancy terms. They don't always provide clarity about what an expert can do for you. More often than not they can create more confusion.

And it doesn't help that sometimes you're not even sure what you need. Your business needs could be a bit fuzzy, like trying to see through a foggy window. It's hard to decide what kind of help you need when the problem itself is unclear.

Now imagine someone striding in with confidence and assurance, claiming they have all the answers. Sounds enticing, doesn't it? But here's a word of caution: real, impactful, valuable expertise doesn't always show up with a set of ready-made answers. The best experts—the ones who can truly make a difference in your business—arrive with more than just answers. They bring with them a trove of incisive questions, proven methodologies, and a commitment to help you uncover your answers.

Choosing an expert to hire isn't about finding a magic bullet. It's about finding a partner, someone who can shine a light on your blind spots, guide you towards clarity, and empower you to make the changes that will drive your business forward. It's not about an "eenie meenie minee mo" choice. It's about a conscious, informed decision that can transform the way you do business.

So, let's delve into how you can navigate this maze, decipher the signposts, see through the fog, and find the right expert for your business.

How to Choose Which Expert to Hire

Choosing the right expert to collaborate with is an art in itself. You may already have a standard checklist or set of criteria in mind, focusing primarily on the area of expertise. Yet selecting the right expert involves more than simply ticking boxes. You must also consider whether the individual or team will be a good fit for your organization.

Here are some additional questions to guide your search:

What Outcomes Do You Want?

To quote Brene Brown, it's time to "paint it done." Rather than vaguely saying, "We want to increase our social following by 15%" or "We want to launch the website," delve deeper into the context around that goal. What do you hope to achieve with it?

Let's think about it in terms of art. Saying you want a picture of trees is broad, but specifying that you want the Bob Ross "happy little trees" flourishing in a Tolkien-inspired fantasy world paints a vivid picture. The same principle applies in business. Contextualize your goals by bringing in the intent behind them.

If you want to increase your social following by 15%, explain why. Is it to maintain your current 2% conversion rate and boost sales revenue from this channel? If you're launching a website, why is that your goal? Is it to provide the sales team with content to prepare prospects to become better clients?

By framing your desired outcomes in this manner, you give potential experts a clear understanding of what you're looking for, enabling them to tailor their services to your unique needs more effectively.

Do you need strategy, planning, implementation, evaluation, or all of the above?

In my experience, it's rare to find one person who excels in all these areas. Usually, it takes a cohesive team to achieve all four effectively. Being clear about what you need can help define project phases and answer the question, "Which expert should you hire?"

Strategists are visionaries who can help you see the bigger picture and set meaningful goals. Planners are detail-oriented individuals who can develop an effective roadmap to achieve those goals.

Implementers are the doers who turn plans into actions, and evaluators are the critical thinkers who assess outcomes and recommend improvements. Depending on your needs, you might want to hire an individual or team that specializes in one or more of these areas.

What does your team want to do? What do they not want to do?

Fostering a harmonious relationship between an external agency and your in-house team is crucial. A common friction point arises when external agencies infringe on the in-house team's territory. By having candid conversations about what the team is eager to do, what they'd rather not handle, and where they're facing capacity constraints, you can better focus the agency's work and facilitate more productive collaboration.

Perhaps your team is eager to brainstorm creative ideas, but would prefer not to manage the logistical details of implementing those ideas. Or maybe your in-house team is great at strategizing and planning, but lacks the technical expertise necessary for implementation. Understanding these nuances can help you choose an expert who complements your team's skills and preferences.

How experienced are you and your team in working with external experts?

Your past experiences can inform your present decision-making. If you and your team have extensive experience working with external agencies, and already have established processes and methods of engagement, you may not need the expert to guide you on how to utilize their services.

However, if you're inexperienced in this area, or if you've had unfavorable experiences in the past, it might be beneficial to find an expert who can bring their own standard operating procedures, engagement, and utilization processes. They can guide you through the collaboration, providing clarity and structure, thus paving the way for a more effective and successful partnership.

It's also worth noting that an expert who has experience with organizations similar to yours, in size, industry, or culture, can often navigate the unique challenges and expectations of your sector more effectively. So, as part of your evaluation process, consider the expert's experience within your specific industry or with similar organizations.

By asking these questions and evaluating the answers thoughtfully, you can enhance your decision-making process, optimizing your chances of finding an expert who not only meets your criteria but also aligns with your organization's culture, needs, and objectives.

Choosing the right expert is about more than expertise—it's about finding someone who can partner with your team to drive your vision forward and help you navigate the ever-evolving business landscape effectively. So remember, take your time, consider these aspects, and make the choice that feels right for you and your organization.

Chapter Six
How to Avoid Hiring the Wrong Expert

*A*voiding the wrong expert or external agency hire is akin to navigating a complex maze. Just like finding the right path towards the right hire, avoiding the pitfalls that lead to the wrong one necessitates having a sound vetting system. This system should bolster your chances of attaining desired outcomes while enabling you to discern potential red flags at an early stage.

While it would be great to have a "magic" process for perfect hiring (spoiler alert: there isn't one), there are essential components you can introduce into your process that significantly enhance your capability to identify a poor fit before it's too late:

1. Don't be in a hurry.

There is a famous saying: "Haste makes waste." When it comes to hiring the right expert, this adage holds a significant degree of truth. Being in a hurry to onboard an expert is a common pitfall that often leads to costly mistakes. A hurried decision can result in overlooking critical warning signs and making choices that are not fully aligned with your needs and goals.

The process of hiring an expert should be deliberate and thoughtful. Most of the time, when the wrong expert was hired warning signs were present. However, these red flags were missed, often because the focus was misplaced on other priorities such as adhering to ambitious timelines. When the hiring process is rushed, it is all too easy to gloss over details that could have signaled potential issues down the line.

Therefore, it is essential to start the hiring process well before you reach a point of crisis. Having ample time allows you to make a comprehensive assessment, thoroughly vet potential candidates, and ultimately make a decision that is well-informed and strategically aligned.

Consider referring back to the chapter on "How to Know When to Hire Experts" for a deeper understanding of the timing and preparations needed before you embark on the hiring journey. There, we discussed how to identify the early signs that you may need an expert and how to prepare your team for the integration of this new skill set. The idea is to plan in advance, not in response to a crisis, to ensure that the expert you bring onboard is the best fit for your needs.

2. Be wary of really polished marketing.

There's an insightful saying from business coach Tara Newman, who astutely observes: "You can tell the real experts by their crappy marketing." Although seemingly counterintuitive, this idea holds an element of truth that warrants serious consideration. As paradoxical as it may sound, an expert's lackluster marketing efforts might indeed indicate their depth of knowledge and dedication to their craft.

First, let's unpack why this may be the case. When someone is truly an expert in their field, they're often deeply immersed in their work, completely consumed by their passion and their craft. This commitment to delivering high-value service can make it challenging for them to step back and dedicate time and effort to marketing their services effectively. Their focus is predominantly on honing their expertise and providing top-notch service to their clients, rather than on creating a polished marketing facade.

Even remarkable marketing agencies can sometimes fall into the trap of the "cobbler's children have no shoes" syndrome. It's a common phenomenon where they're so preoccupied with delivering excellent work for their clients that they neglect their own marketing needs. Their website may appear outdated or their LinkedIn profiles incomplete, not because they lack skills or capabilities but because they prioritize their clients' work over their own.

This isn't to say that you should only consider experts with poorly designed websites or incomplete profiles. Quite the contrary, you should keep an open mind. If you encounter an expert whose marketing isn't top-notch, don't discount them immediately. Instead, it might be worth taking the time to engage in a conversation with them. You may find that beneath their unpolished exterior lies a wealth of knowledge and expertise.

However, it's crucial to note that quality services can indeed have great marketing. Stellar marketing shouldn't automatically be viewed with suspicion, but it should be a signal to be extra diligent in your evaluation process. It can be tempting to get drawn in by flashy websites, polished portfolios, and compelling testimonials. But remember, these elements, while important, are only parts of the bigger picture.

While great marketing can indicate a company's understanding of its audience and its ability to present its offerings appealingly, it shouldn't overshadow the value of substantive experience, expertise, and results. If you encounter a provider with a polished marketing presence, ensure that the shine isn't just surface-level.

Do they have a track record of delivering results? Can they provide client references or case studies? Do they have subject matter expertise, and can they communicate complex concepts in a clear and understandable way? Are they responsive to your inquiries, and do they display a deep understanding of your unique problems and needs?

By being cautious and conducting thorough due diligence, you can help ensure that you're not just enamored by an expert's polished marketing, but that you're hiring an expert with the substance and expertise to back it up.

3. Use your core values to evaluate potential experts.

Aligning your business decisions with your organization's core values is crucial in all aspects of operations, and the process of hiring an expert is no exception. Your core values are the guiding principles that represent what your organization stands for, and they should play a pivotal role in evaluating potential experts.

Much like when you're looking to expand your in-house team, using your core values to vet potential experts can be an effective litmus test for compatibility and early identification of any incongruities. The goal is not merely to find an expert with the right skills and knowledge, but to find one who will also mesh well with your organization's culture and ethos.

In our own practice, the first conversation we have with any potential partner, vendor, or team member revolves around our core values. We invite them to explore these values, ask for their impressions, and inquire about which values, if any, resonate with them. Their feedback in this conversation can be incredibly telling.

If a prospective expert doesn't engage in this discussion, doesn't provide feedback or share any thoughts about your values, that's a red flag. For instance, one of our core values is "Give a Damn." If a potential expert displays indifference or disinterest when discussing our values, they're clearly not aligned with the ethos encapsulated in "Give a Damn."

Aligning with values from the get-go serves as a preventive measure, ensuring that you're not engaging with experts operating from a different basis or fundamentally different philosophy. A disconnect here can lead to misunderstandings, miscommunications, and even conflicts down the line.

Remember, experts are not just service providers; they become an extension of your team during the project. They will interact with your team members, represent your organization in various contexts, and influence decision-making processes. It's therefore essential that their values align with yours.

In the grand scheme of things, a professional relationship built on shared values is more likely to foster mutual understanding, smooth collaboration, and a fruitful partnership. It sets the stage for seamless communication, shared decision-making and, ultimately, successful project outcomes.

So make sure to let your organization's core values lead the way in your evaluation process. This will allow you to go beyond surface-level considerations and select an expert who's not just competent, but also a perfect fit for your organization's culture and value system.

4. Does your communication style match their communication style?

Effective communication plays an integral role in the successful engagement with external experts. An expert may have top-tier knowledge and experience, but if they can't communicate effectively with you and your team it can become a major barrier to productivity and successful outcomes. It's therefore essential to ensure that your communication style aligns with that of the expert you're considering.

One important facet of communication is content—the actual message being communicated. Can the expert convey complex concepts in a manner that's easy for your team to understand? Some highly technical experts can get lost in industry jargon and technical language that can be hard to grasp for those outside their field. If your expert can't translate their expertise into plain, understandable language, it can lead to confusion and frustration. It's like they're speaking a foreign language, one that your team can't understand. So look for an expert who can bridge this gap effectively.

But there's more to communication than just content. The choice of communication channels, the context of communication, and the connection that comes with it are equally important.

Consider the channels through which communication will happen. Does your organization predominantly use Slack while your expert primarily uses email? Maybe the expert has a preference for Notion while your team is accustomed to SharePoint. A mismatch in communication channels can lead to a disconnection, miscommunication, and unnecessary friction in the collaboration process.

Understanding the preferred communication channels of both parties allows you to anticipate potential challenges and plan for solutions. If you can determine this in the early stages of engagement, it gives you a head start in addressing potential obstacles.

Keep in mind, an effective partnership isn't just about working together; it's about communicating together. A shared understanding facilitated by a mutual communication style builds trust, reduces misunderstandings, and promotes successful collaboration. So as you vet potential experts, be sure to consider whether their communication style aligns with yours. This alignment can make all the difference in ensuring smooth and successful collaboration.

5. Tune in to their ability to listen.

One of the most crucial attributes an expert or external agency should possess is the ability to listen effectively. Many organizations and individuals may believe they understand the problem at hand, but the best external agencies and experts often have a knack for uncovering underlying issues or unanticipated opportunities that may have been overlooked. This discovery requires a honed ability to listen, comprehend, and then ask the right questions to delve deeper into the matter.

Remember, conversations with potential experts should not resemble a monologue, but rather a dialogue where the exchange of ideas, perspectives, and insights takes place. This isn't limited to the initial discovery or briefing stage; it should permeate all stages of your engagement.

Consider this: if your potential expert spends 90% of your conversation presenting their skills, qualifications, or past work without giving ample room for understanding your unique situation and goals, it's a warning sign. They might be excellent in their field, but if they're not tuned in to your specific needs it might suggest a lack of customization in their approach. There's a risk they might attempt to apply a one-size-fits-all solution that may not perfectly align with your specific requirements or situation.

The real value of experts comes from their ability to tailor their expertise to your unique needs, and this demands a deep understanding of your issues, context, and goals. This understanding can only come from asking thoughtful, probing questions and genuinely listening to your responses.

If the expert you're considering asks incisive questions and devotes at least 50% of your conversations to listening, these are promising indicators. They suggest the expert or agency is truly invested in understanding your needs, which can significantly increase the chances of them delivering a solution that fits like a glove. Remember, in the realm of expertise there's no substitute for a genuine willingness and ability to listen.

As you consider potential experts or agencies to work with, be sure to tune in to their ability to listen. It's a subtle skill, but it can make a world of difference in determining the success of your engagement.

6. Does the expert have a defined process or framework to guide the project or work?

The presence of a defined process or framework can often signal the quality and depth of an expert's experience. Such a framework serves as a roadmap that allows the expert to navigate the complexities of your project, step-by-step, ensuring nothing falls through the cracks. It's akin to a well-tested recipe that the expert can follow, tweak, and adapt based on the unique flavors and ingredients of your organization and its needs.

If your potential expert lacks a process or a framework, it may suggest they're more of an executor than a strategist. They might be adept at taking instructions and implementing solutions, but they may not excel at strategizing, planning, or consulting. If you only need an executor, that's perfectly fine. However, if you need more, it's essential to know this early on to ensure a successful match.

Quality processes and frameworks aren't rigid constructs. They are flexible and adaptable systems designed to assimilate input from your organization, helping the expert to shape their approach accordingly. The best experts are those who blend their standardized procedures with the unique circumstances, culture, and needs of your organization. They understand that, while processes bring structure and efficiency, each client's situation demands a unique approach.

A clearly defined process or framework also brings transparency, allowing you to understand what you should expect at each stage of the engagement. This can reduce ambiguity, set appropriate expectations, and foster a healthy, collaborative working relationship.

So, when considering a potential expert or external agency, ask them about their processes or frameworks. This will not only provide you with a glimpse into their way of working but will also help you assess if their approach aligns with what you need for your project or work. Remember, the right expert is not just about the right skills but also about the right process.

7. Keep your scorecards in mind.

As the adage goes, "What gets measured, gets managed." This wisdom holds true even when hiring an expert or an external agency. Scorecards offer a structured approach to measure the success of a project and thus are a valuable tool when determining the best fit for your needs.

You may recall our discussion on scorecards in the chapter "How to Know When to Hire Experts." If you are new to the concept, a scorecard is a tangible, structured framework that defines the key performance indicators (KPIs) and the desired outcomes of a project. These could range from quantifiable metrics such as revenue growth, customer engagement, or on-time delivery, to more qualitative aspects like improvement in team morale, enhancement in brand perception, or growth in strategic capabilities.

By having your scorecards in mind right from the start, you align your expectations with your expert's offerings. You'll be able to gauge whether their skills and experiences match the metrics you're aiming to improve. It allows you to communicate your expectations more effectively, and sets a clear benchmark for what success looks like.

In essence, keeping your scorecards in mind gives you an analytical tool to evaluate prospective experts, ensuring that their capabilities align with your strategic objectives. It's about being intentional and objective in your hiring decision, thus further safeguarding your organization against the pitfalls of hiring the wrong expert.

The Benefits of Hiring Well

The decision to hire an expert or external agency is a significant one, with far-reaching implications for your organization. Get it right, and you open up a world of possibilities—solutions to complex problems, fresh perspectives, advanced skills, and valuable partnerships. Get it wrong, and you face a maelstrom of wasted resources, missed opportunities, frustration, and potential burnout.

Our exploration of how to avoid hiring the wrong expert has underscored the importance of a measured and thoughtful approach to the hiring process. We've delved into essential components to consider in the hiring process, from avoiding haste and aligning core values, to evaluating communication styles and processes, and keeping scorecards in mind. While the process may appear complex, the rewards of careful, calculated decision-making are truly worthwhile.

Hiring the right expert is a value-adding proposition. It is not just about meeting immediate needs, but also about investing in your organization's future. Hiring well means you invite individuals or entities into your team that can significantly enhance your capacity, improve your performance, and potentially transform the way you operate. They become trusted partners and advisors whose expertise and insights can shape your strategy, drive innovation, and help you navigate the complexities of your business environment. The right experts do not merely fulfill a function. They integrate with your team, understand your culture, and work towards your shared objectives.

Furthermore, by avoiding bad hires you conserve precious time and resources. Every wrong hire is a drain on your budget, a potential source of friction within your team, and a distraction from your core mission. Worse still, a bad hiring experience can create a climate of mistrust and reluctance to seek external help in the future. It's a situation that can lead to overburdening your team, creating stress and potential burnout.

Yet this doesn't have to be your narrative. By approaching the hiring process with clear-eyed pragmatism, armed with the strategies we've discussed, you can sidestep these pitfalls. You can build successful collaborations with experts who propel your organization towards its goals. These fruitful partnerships are the antidote to the isolationist impulse to do it yourself when faced with challenges beyond your team's capacity. They affirm the power of collaboration, the value of external perspectives, and the potential for synergistic growth when you combine your in-house capabilities with external expertise.

Now, having equipped you with the knowledge of how to avoid hiring the wrong expert, it's time to shift our focus to preparing your organization for the work to begin. How do you set the stage for a successful collaboration with your expert? How can you ensure a smooth integration of their skills and insights into your organization? How do you navigate the dynamics of working with an external entity? These are the questions we will address in our journey ahead. So stay tuned, keep your notepad handy, and prepare for the next phase of our exploration.

Chapter Seven
Preparing Your Organization to Work with an Expert

There is an inherent wisdom in the saying, "Success loves preparation." In our quest to tap into the transformative potential of external expertise, preparation emerges as a critical factor. It's not just about identifying the right expert or avoiding the wrong hire; it's about priming your organization to extract maximum value from this engagement.

To truly harness the power of external expertise, you need to set the stage from the outset. As soon as the thought of enlisting expert help crosses your mind, the process of preparation should begin. This isn't about drafting contracts or setting project milestones; it's about fostering a readiness to learn, adapt, and change even before the expert steps into the scene.

And here's the reality: change is challenging. This fact is woven into the fabric of human nature and magnified within the complex web of organizational dynamics. As we engage experts for their transformative potential, we inadvertently sign up for a journey of change. Now, this journey is not always smooth. It can be fraught with misunderstandings, resistance, and unforeseen obstacles. Yet with the right preparation these hurdles can be transformed into stepping stones towards successful engagements.

Throughout this book, a recurring theme may have started to resonate: experts are not omniscient. They are brilliant at what they do, masters of their specific domain. But expecting them to be experts in everything, including how to integrate seamlessly into your organization, is not only unrealistic but also a potential recipe for disappointment.

An expert might have profound knowledge in their field and the capacity to deliver high-value services. However, their ability to communicate their expertise, make it accessible to your team, and navigate the nuances of your organization's culture is a different skill set altogether. This is where your role in preparing your organization becomes paramount.

I've seen many instances where organizations, despite having secured the services of a highly skilled expert, didn't receive the value they anticipated. The reason was often a misalignment between the expert's approach and the organization's readiness to absorb and implement their insights. It wasn't a reflection of the expert's competence but rather a consequence of inadequate preparation on the organization's part.

Sometimes, it might not be clear where things went awry. The engagement could be marked by subtle inefficiencies that add up over time, creating a gap between expectations and reality.

In other cases, the pitfalls might be glaringly evident—resistance to new ideas, communication breakdowns, or misaligned objectives. Regardless of the form it takes, the result is the same: lost opportunities and diminished value.

This underscores the importance of laying the groundwork for effective collaboration with experts. Your organization must be equipped not only to benefit from the expert's knowledge but also to facilitate their understanding of your unique context. Remember, experts bring with them a wealth of skills and experiences, but they might not inherently know how to mesh perfectly with your organization. This is where your preparation comes into play.

Preparing Unlocks Easy

The old adage "preparation is key" is especially true when it comes to working with experts. The purpose of prep work, whether it's in the kitchen, the paint studio, or the business world, is to make the actual engagement go smoothly. However, this process often gets overshadowed by the final output, making it seem less significant than it really is.

Let's illustrate this with a rather tasty example. Have you ever watched a cooking show and wondered how they make it look so easy? My favorite is The Pioneer Woman. When I watch her whip up a mouthwatering casserole or hearty breakfast, it appears seamless, almost like a beautiful dance in the kitchen. But let's hit pause for a moment. The reality is, it looks that way because there's a well-oiled machine working tirelessly behind the scenes.

There's an entire crew that has already shopped for the ingredients, measured them out (often in those adorable little glass bowls that I certainly don't own), and preheated the oven before the cameras even start rolling. It's the culmination of this meticulous prep work that allows our beloved Pioneer Woman to deliver culinary magic on screen. This is exactly the case when you prepare your organization to work with an expert.

Now let's dip our brushes into another analogy. I'll be candid—I despise painting. Not so much the actual painting process with its transformative power to change an entire room or house, but the excruciating prep work it necessitates. There's the whole ordeal of sanding down the surfaces, applying masking tape with surgical precision, removing items from the walls, making repairs where needed, and laying down tarps to protect your precious furniture. It's a Herculean task, and just like preparing for an expert it's a critical precursor to a job well done.

Moving into the realm of business, let's consider the role of a tax accountant. I think they have one of the toughest gigs around when it comes to preparing their clients for engagement. They need a veritable mountain of information to do their job effectively. This usually entails details that are hidden in the client's deepest crevices, making the process feel like a never-ending treasure hunt. But without this data, tax accountants simply can't function at their best. And let's face it, it's virtually impossible for them to retrieve this information independently, especially when the client's filing system is comprised of shoeboxes stuffed with receipts!

These examples illuminate the vital yet underappreciated role that prep work plays in any project. This principle holds true when engaging with an expert.

Admittedly, preparation can be a hassle, sometimes even a thorn in our sides. But haven't we all been part of projects where the prep work was either neglected or haphazardly executed? And how did those endeavors turn out? More often than not they deviated from the original plan, ran over budget, and left us feeling shortchanged. I mean, imagine finding bugs permanently immortalized in your freshly painted windowsill because nobody bothered to clean it beforehand—yuck!

In a nutshell, preparation, although seemingly tedious and time-consuming, lays the foundation for success. When you properly prepare your organization for an expert's engagement, you're not just setting the stage for a smooth operation but also ensuring that you extract the maximum value from the expert's contribution. So while it might seem tempting to rush through or skip this process, remember the bugs on the windowsill. The stakes are too high and the benefits of thorough preparation are too significant to ignore.

Create a Smart Prep Plan

There is good news, though. The heavy lifting of preparing to engage with an expert or external team isn't a never-ending cycle. Once you've climbed this mountain and crafted a method to your madness, you've essentially paved the way for smoother collaborations in the future. This initial investment of effort and time will bear fruit each time you need to onboard an expert thereafter. Simply dust off your prep blueprint and deploy it.

And let's be real here. Every organization is as unique as a fingerprint, and there's no one-size-fits-all approach when it comes to prepping for an expert. Your organization is a beautiful mosaic of different personalities, talents, strengths, and weaknesses. It's a blend of varying levels of maturity and experience. It's a complex web of intricacies that makes it distinct. And this uniqueness calls for a tailor-made prep plan to maximize the engagement with an expert.

However, this doesn't mean you have to create everything from scratch. The key is to develop your own framework or formula, a bespoke roadmap to help you navigate the prep work effectively. And to kickstart this process, I'm going to share a set of prompts and questions that act as your North Star.

Think of these as guiding lights that illuminate your path, helping you tailor a preparation strategy that fits your organization like a well-tailored suit. The goal here is not to offer you a rigid instruction manual but rather a flexible guide that you can modify and adapt to your organization's unique needs. Because at the end of the day, a well-crafted prep plan is not just about ticking off a checklist; it's about embracing a strategic mindset, understanding the nuances of your organization, and facilitating a meaningful collaboration with the expert.

Crafting a Vivid Vision: Painting It Done

One critical component of creating your prep plan is visualization or, as we've referred to before, "Painting It Done." It's all about outlining the expected outcome of the project in vivid detail. Yes, we've mentioned this before in the chapter "How To Choose Which Expert To Hire." In fact, this is so important it's worth repeating. Not just for choosing the right expert, but also for preparing your team to work with them effectively.

This preparation phase is like setting the stage for a grand play. It's not just about determining the end scene but also about understanding the twists and turns of the plot that would lead to the grand finale. It's the time to gather your team and draft the whole narrative, from "Here's the result we want" to "Here's how it's going to be used." Go beyond the surface level and dive into the intricate details: "Here's what didn't work last time," "Here's the context," "Here are the pain points."

You want to paint a vibrant, detailed picture that's teeming with color and nuance. You want to capture the entirety of the story, the triumphs and tribulations, the hits and misses, the context and the complexities. Think of it as your project blue-print—a comprehensive depiction that encapsulates everything needed to turn the result into a resounding success.

Why is this so important? Three words: clarity, cohesiveness, and alignment. These are the magic ingredients you'll need as you start working with your expert. They are the foundations of effective collaboration, ensuring everyone's on the same page, striving towards the same goal, and sharing the same vi-sion. So dust off your artistic skills and start painting your pro-ject done, because a well-defined vision is half the battle won.

Demystifying the Deliverables: Let's Define Them

The second component of the preparation process involves de-fining the deliverables. Now, you may be thinking, "Wait a minute, we don't even know what deliverables we need yet." And you know what? That's perfectly okay! Uncertainty is a part and parcel of the initial stages of any project.

Acknowledging that there are gaps in your knowledge and un-derstanding (hello, Dunning-Kruger effect!) is a big step for-ward. It's a testament to your self-awareness and ability to rec-ognize that you need expert assistance to navigate this terrain. So don't see this as a stumbling block, but rather as an oppor-tunity to invite experts to step in and fill those gaps. That's what they're there for, after all!

Incorporating this step into your prep plan serves a dual pur-pose.

First, it ensures that no crucial aspect is overlooked. Often in the rush of starting a project, defining deliverables can become a mere afterthought. But it's essential to outline what the end product should look like, what milestones should be reached, and what benchmarks should be hit. These details provide structure and a clear roadmap for your project.

Second, it gives voice to the needs and expectations of your organization. By detailing your needs, even if they're not fully fleshed out, you're paving the way for a more open, transparent conversation with the experts you intend to hire. It allows them to understand your requirements better and thus tailor their expertise to meet your specific needs.

So even if you're not entirely sure about what you need, start sketching out the deliverables. The picture will become clearer as you delve deeper into the project, and your expert will be there to add the finishing touches. Remember, a well-defined deliverable is the first step towards a successful project completion.

Unraveling the Process: What Do You Expect?

Sometimes, we bring on experts to fill the shoes of their predecessors, and that comes with its own set of expected processes. Maybe these processes were originally established by you, or perhaps they were put in place by the outgoing agency or expert. Regardless of their origins there's an understanding that something's going to happen, some sort of rhythm that's expected to continue.

So if you find yourself in this situation, it's time to take a step back and really analyze this process. What does it involve? How has it worked in the past? Are there any areas for improvement, or is it working like a well-oiled machine?

Once you've pondered these questions, put pen to paper (or fingers to keyboard). Document these expectations. Sketch out the steps, outline the timelines, indicate the milestones, and highlight the deliverables. Provide as much detail as you can.

Why is this necessary, you ask? Well, it all boils down to clear communication. When you hire an external expert or agency, you'll need to make them aware of your expectations right from the outset. This could mean that they'll have to adapt to your set process, or they may suggest changes to streamline and improve the existing system.

But no matter which direction you choose to take, it's crucial that expectations are brought to the forefront. Transparency in this regard ensures a smoother transition, helps avoid misunderstandings, and sets the foundation for a successful partnership. So don't shy away from clarifying your process expectations—it's an integral part of preparing to work with an expert.

Anticipating the Roadblocks: Identifying Potential Hiccups and Solutions

One of the most familiar issues that may arise during your engagement with an expert revolves around the perennial problem: communication. Experts, due to their highly specialized knowledge and technical acumen, may inadvertently create a disconnect. It's not that they're being intentionally opaque, but sometimes their level of comprehension can be miles apart from yours. They might be gazing at the stars while you're trying to build the rocket.

The best policy for communication with an expert is the same for really any relationship: Don't assume, and communicate early and often.

In other instances, the fault might not lie with the expert. Perhaps your organization failed to prepare sufficiently, or didn't adequately factor in the timing of the engagement in conjunction with other demands on your team or organization. These scenarios can set the stage for stumbling blocks that might trip up the entire project.

So how do you navigate around these potential pitfalls? Start by conducting a thorough debrief or retrospect of your recent engagements with experts. Where did the typical issues crop up? Was there a pattern to these hiccups? Can you discern any tangible or intangible factors that could have precipitated these issues? If these problems were to occur again, what could you do differently to prevent or at least minimize them?

To deepen your understanding, you could also flip the question and ask, "What is it that we don't want?" This helps clarify what kind of challenges you would prefer to avoid. It's just as important to know what you're steering clear of as it is to know where you're heading.

Remember, no project runs entirely smoothly, and it's normal to encounter roadblocks along the way. The key is in foreseeing these potential issues and preparing for them. By doing this, you'll significantly reduce the friction in your collaboration with experts, allowing you to extract the maximum value from their expertise.

Setting the Boundaries: Laying Out the Rules of Engagement

The power of clarity cannot be overemphasized, particularly when it comes to defining the rules of engagement. These rules, either explicitly stated or implicitly understood, form the foundation for smooth collaboration. They're like the guardrails on a highway, preventing your project from veering off course.

Your organization, like every other, is a unique entity with its own hierarchy and cultural norms. It might be a strict top-down structure, or it might be a free-wheeling, innovative start-up environment. Whatever it may be, it's crucial to lay this out for the expert. Have previous experts tripped up over any unexpected organizational quirks? Being upfront about these instances will help your newly-hired expert steer clear of making the same mistakes.

Equipping your expert with a comprehensive understanding of your organization's structure and culture is akin to giving them a detailed map. Who are the key stakeholders? Who wields the decision-making power? Are there any territorial lines drawn around certain areas of ownership? What about any sensitive issues or projects that require a more delicate approach? All of this information will arm your expert with the knowledge they need to navigate your organization effectively and efficiently.

By setting clear boundaries and defining the rules of engagement, you're essentially streamlining the process for your expert. With a thorough understanding of how things work within your organization, they can focus their energy and time on delivering the maximum value to your project. This clarity reduces misunderstandings and confusion, paving the way for a fruitful and harmonious collaboration.

The Sweet Taste of Success: The Benefits of Prepping to Work with an Expert

Stepping into the kitchen armed with a well-prepared recipe, measured ingredients, and a clear plan of action, you're far more likely to whip up a gastronomic delight that mirrors the glossy image on the recipe card. Now translate this culinary scenario to the realm of business and project management.

When your organization does the necessary groundwork to work effectively with an expert, it's like setting the stage for a well-choreographed performance. Your prep work mirrors the mise en place in a professional kitchen. You've considered all aspects, from identifying clear outcomes to defining deliverables, setting expectations, and laying out the rules of engagement.

On the other hand, your expert comes prepared with their own set of skills, experiences, and strategies. It's like they've brought the secret sauce, the exotic spices, or the unique cooking technique.

When both parties come to the table prepared, that's when the magic happens. Like a chef expertly blending ingredients to create a stunning dish, your project starts to take shape. It's faster because you're not scrambling to figure out what needs to be done. It's smoother because you've anticipated potential issues and prepared for them. And the end result is exactly what you hoped for, if not better!

By doing your due diligence you're ensuring a well-cooked meal, not a half-baked idea. The time and effort invested in preparing your organization to work with an expert will reap dividends. It allows you to savor the process and enjoy the outcome—a successful project that's akin to the delicious dish pictured on the recipe card. So go ahead, do your prep work and get ready to relish the flavor of success!

Chapter Eight
How to Work
with Experts

Roll out the red carpet, folks, because it's showtime! We've set the stage, the script is ready, and it's time to let the stars of our show, the experts, step into the limelight and do what they do best.

But wait, before we get too carried away with our Hollywood metaphors, let's make sure we're clear about one thing. This is not about simply sitting back, kicking your feet up, and watching the experts work their magic. Well, not entirely. As we've seen in the previous chapters, effectively engaging and working with an expert is a dance. It requires a well-orchestrated balance of preparation, communication, and collaboration. And even when the expert is doing their thing, there is still a role for you to play.

In this chapter we'll delve into the nitty-gritty of how to truly get the most value from working with an expert. More specifically, we'll talk about how you can provide an environment where your experts can thrive and deliver their best work.

We'll cover what it means to engage your expert effectively, how to maintain a harmonious working relationship, and some common pitfalls to avoid. Plus, we'll wrap it all up with a case study to showcase the significant benefits of getting it right.

Beginning with the End in Mind Provides a Huge Payoff

Just like planning a journey, it's smart to know your destination before you start your engines. When it comes to expert-client relationships, that means thinking about offboarding even when you're just getting started. It may seem a little backward, but trust me, it makes things a lot smoother down the line. Let's break it down, shall we?

The beauty of keeping the end in mind from the beginning is that it creates a sort of road map for the entire engagement. You're essentially prepping for the exit while still enjoying the ride. It's an organized approach that allows both parties to make the most of their time together while also setting up for a smooth departure.

For you as a client, this method is a time and effort saver. Imagine not having to scramble at the last minute, not having to fire off a barrage of questions or requests for explanations to the expert post-engagement. It's about retaining all that precious value you've invested in during the relationship. No lost documents, no misplaced assets, and definitely no losing sleep over not being able to continue the work post-offboarding. It's about securing your investment and ensuring a smooth transition.

For the expert, starting with the end in mind is also beneficial. It ensures their time and resources are spent most efficiently, not only during the engagement but also when it's time to wrap things up. It's about wrapping up the relationship in a professional, clean, and respectful manner, without the need for last-minute scrambles or undue extensions.

When you put it all together, beginning with the end in mind equips both you and the expert to handle the relationship's eventual end with grace and ease. It's like drafting a prenuptial agreement before a marriage. Sure, it might not sound like the most romantic proposition, but it provides clarity, sets expectations, and shields against any unforeseen circumstances. You hope you'll never need it, but it's comforting to know it's there.

So as you embark on your journey with an expert, bear in mind where you'll eventually wind up. It's a little like driving backwards, but once you get the hang of it, it offers a huge payoff in the long run. Because when you start with the end in mind, the journey becomes all the more worthwhile.

Engaging Your Expert

We've arrived at the big moment—time to bring our expert onboard. Now, if you're thinking this means just handing over the reins to your expert and saying, "Alright, do your thing" think again. Engaging an expert isn't about dropping them into the deep end and hoping they swim. It's about setting them up for success. Here's how to do that.

First things first. Most experts worth their salt will have a well-structured onboarding process in place. This procedure often involves a series of initial meetings, data collection, and a thorough review of your current situation. Their aim is to get up to speed with your project, organization, or the specific challenges they're being hired to address. This is good news. It means you're dealing with a professional who understands the importance of doing their homework.

But don't get too comfortable just yet. You also have an essential part to play here. Remember all that preparation work we did in the last chapter? Well, here's where it pays off. Your prep work wasn't just for show; it was to arm your expert with as much relevant information and context as possible. This can range from the history of the project, any previous attempts or failures, the intended goal, key stakeholders, and more. Essentially, anything that can help them understand what they're stepping into and how success will be measured.

Think of this as creating a quick reference guide for your expert. It doesn't need to be a hundred-page document or an elaborate PowerPoint presentation. It could be as simple as a checklist, a one-pager, or a few talking points to bring up in your initial kick-off meeting. The aim here is to save your expert from wading through heaps of information and instead provide a concise, targeted overview that helps them hit the ground running.

If you're an organization that regularly works with external experts or freelancers, it might be worth investing in a more formal onboarding process. Something that systematically provides them with the necessary connections, access, and information needed to smoothly integrate into your workflow. This could involve introductions to key team members, granting access to relevant systems or databases, and sharing any crucial project documentation.

Engaging your expert effectively means more than just hiring them and leaving them to it. It means actively setting them up for success, providing them with all the tools and information they need, and maintaining open, clear communication from the get-go. Remember, you and your expert are partners in this dance. It's your shared responsibility to make it a memorable one. So let's get started on the right foot, shall we?

Working Well Together: The Cha-Cha of Expert Engagement

Okay, so you've done your homework, hired an expert, and set your expectations. High fives all around! Now comes the really exciting part: the actual engagement. It's time to roll up your sleeves and work together to create something truly spectacular.

But here's the catch. Working well together is often easier said than done. In this dance, you and your expert are partners, stepping and twirling around the ballroom floor, trying to keep in time with the music. If one of you misses a beat or steps on the other's toes, it can throw the whole performance off.

Now I'm not saying you have to be a pro dancer to work well with an expert (though that would make board meetings a lot more interesting!). What I am saying is that you need to lead, follow and, most importantly, communicate effectively. That's the secret sauce that's going to turn your engagement from a clumsy shuffle to a polished foxtrot.

To successfully drive the project and create an effective working relationship, there are three key areas of focus:

1. **Leadership** - Identifying who will take the lead in this engagement is a crucial early step. Depending on the situation, it could be you driving the project, or the expert leading the charge. This decision sets the tone for your collaboration.

2. **Structure** - More than numbers and plans, structure refers to the framework that allows for regular communication and progress checks. A well-set structure provides the stability needed to build a productive engagement.

3. **Expectations** - These are an ongoing part of the project. Expectations will need to be reassessed and updated as the project progresses. With clear and mutually-understood expectations, your professional dance can flow smoothly and elegantly, avoiding stepping-on-toes and tripping.

Working well together isn't just about getting the job done. It's about building relationships, growing together, and achieving something truly remarkable. So grab your dancing shoes and let's make some magic happen!

Decide Upfront Who Is Going to Lead: Navigating the Power Dynamics

There's an important conversation that is often overlooked when engaging with an expert, and it's all about leadership. This isn't about a power trip or asserting dominance; it's about clearly defining roles and expectations from the start to avoid any confusion down the line.

Let's be real here. Experts come in all shapes and sizes, with myriad different skill sets and experiences under their belt. You might be hiring a whiz-kid freelancer who can code CSS like they were born to do it, or perhaps it's a seasoned marketing guru with years of industry knowledge. Regardless of who they are and what they bring to the table, it's important to define who is going to lead the project.

In some cases, it may be you. Maybe you've got the bigger picture in mind, and you need this expert to execute a particular aspect. That's perfectly fine. Just ensure this is communicated from the get-go. And while you're leading, remember that you hired this expert for a reason. They possess specialized knowledge and experience that you don't. So even if you're holding the reins, are you making room for their expertise?

It's all too easy to get caught up in the driver's seat and forget to ask for directions. But we need to remember that these experts aren't just here to nod and carry out orders. They're here to provide insights, advice, and potential solutions we might not have considered. So are you making space for their feedback? Are you inviting them to contribute their ideas and expertise?

Moreover, are you providing a clear picture of the desired end result? Providing a crystal-clear vision of the outcome you want is critical. Not only does this give your expert a target to aim for, but it also allows them to leverage their expertise to suggest the best path to reach that goal.

So whether you're taking the lead or delegating the leadership to your expert, remember this: leadership isn't about control. It's about guiding the project towards success while maximizing the value of everyone involved. And that includes your expert.

Structure Matters: The Power of Organized Engagement

If there's one thing I've learned over the years, it's this: structure matters. It's the invisible scaffolding that holds everything together and keeps us moving in the right direction. Without it, things can quickly turn chaotic and unproductive, and that's the last thing any of us wants when working with an expert.

There might be times when you don't want to be involved in the minutiae of the project. Maybe you have other pressing tasks, or perhaps you want to step back and let the expert take control. After all, you hired them because they're great at what they do, right? And that's absolutely okay! It's possible to take a step back without letting go of the reins completely.

How, you might ask? Well, your responsibility then shifts towards defining clear objectives, timelines, and outcomes. It's like being a GPS: your role is to give accurate directions and leave the driving to them. It's important that your expert knows exactly what you expect of them, when you expect it, and what the finished product should look like.

Alongside this, make sure to establish a structure for regular check-ins and communication. Set up periodic meetings to discuss progress, solve any problems, and keep the project on track. This could be weekly emails, bi-weekly conference calls, or even monthly face-to-face meetings, depending on the nature of the project and your relationship with the expert.

With this structure in place you can comfortably step back, knowing that you'll remain informed about the project's status. The only time you'll need to roll up your sleeves and dig in deeper is if the milestones or check-ins aren't being met.

So remember, while the expert is doing their magic, your role is to provide a solid structure that supports their work and steers the project towards its successful conclusion.

In addition to the structure of roles and responsibilities, there is also the systems structure to consider. Understanding how your organization requires information to be structured and the systems in use allows you to have your expert work in your systems, or at least provide their work in ways that can be integrated into your existing systems. See more about management systems in the chapter "Offboarding is as Important as Onboarding."

Setting (and Re-setting) Expectations: The Guide to Smooth Sailing

Ah, expectations. Our frequent companions, and often our harshest critics. Anne Lamott once said, "Expectations are resentments waiting to happen" and boy, was she on to something. But here's a twist: when it comes to professional engagements, expectations aren't just inevitable; they're actually essential.

Think about it. Whether it's a home renovation, a new marketing campaign, or a software development project, the key to success is having clear expectations. And that means doing more than just setting them at the beginning. It means voicing them, updating them, writing them down and, most importantly, communicating them often.

See, here's the thing about expectations: they're not set in stone. As the project evolves, so will your expectations. Maybe the scope has broadened, or a deadline has shifted. Maybe new stakeholders have come onboard. These changes need to be communicated clearly to your expert so they can adjust their work accordingly. Again, communicate early and often.

And when you hit a bump in the road? Revisit those expectations. Friction, issues, conflicts—these are often signs that expectations have been misaligned or misunderstood. Use these moments as opportunities to realign, to ensure that you, your team, and your expert are all on the same page.

In the end, a well-managed relationship with your expert aligns closely with the results you want to achieve. Everyone involved should have a shared understanding of the outcome, the timelines, and the route to get there. So set those expectations, keep them fluid, and communicate, communicate, communicate. It's your compass for a smooth and successful journey.

Big Finish

You've sashayed through the dance of leadership, waltzed around the structure, and even tangoed with expectations. That deserves a well-earned standing ovation, don't you think?

In all seriousness, if you've been keeping up with this journey, you should be well-equipped to work harmoniously with your expert. Remember, this isn't just a one-and-done operation; it's a dance that evolves and changes with the music (or in our case, the scope of the project).

Every step you take in this engagement dance—whether it's deciding who leads, structuring your work process, or setting and adjusting expectations—is pivotal in ensuring a smooth and fruitful collaboration. It's all about rhythm, communication, and flexibility. When these elements work in sync, it's like a well-orchestrated waltz that leads to a magnificent performance. Or, in our context, the successful realization of your project goals.

As we wrap up this section, keep in mind that every dance may have its stumbles, and every engagement its hurdles. But that's all part of the journey. As long as you're learning, adapting, and continuously fine-tuning your dance steps, you're on the right path.

Working well together is a rewarding dance that leads to growth, innovation and, most importantly, achieving something extraordinary.

Issues to Avoid

Entering the world of professional collaboration, especially with experts, can sometimes be tricky, like navigating an intricate maze. You want to reach the end goal successfully, but there are a few stumbling blocks along the way you'd prefer to avoid.

This section, in many ways, is your guide to this maze. We'll be shining a light on three pitfalls that often show up when working with experts: The Steam Roller, Micromanagement, and Lack of Clarity. It's important to note that these issues are usually unintended consequences of our own actions. After all, no one starts a project with the intention to steamroll, micromanage, or be vague.

"Beware the Steam Roller" speaks to the importance of not overwhelming or overpowering our experts with our ideas or processes. "Banish Micromanagement" emphasizes the significance of giving the expert space to work in their domain. Lastly, "Clear is Kind" underlines the vital role of clear communication and setting well-defined expectations.

By recognizing these potential issues, we can mitigate them effectively and create a more harmonious working environment for everyone involved. The goal here is to foster a space where experts can fully utilize their skills and experience, ultimately leading to successful project completion.

Beware the Steam Roller

Experts are like heavy machinery. They're built to handle big jobs. They're designed to take on tasks that are too heavy or too specialized for others. However, as robust as they are, they can't function properly if they're not allowed to do what they're best at. Enter the "Steam Roller" scenario. It's a metaphorical beast that can take an expert's productivity and grind it to a halt.

Picture this: you've hired an expert to lend their knowledge and skills to your organization. You've identified a gap in your organization's capabilities, and you've sourced the right person to bridge that gap. But somewhere along the line you find yourself talking more than listening, driving the project in the direction you see fit, overshadowing the expert's input. You're unintentionally steam rolling over your expert's ability to contribute their unique value to your project.

Now, let's be clear. This isn't about blame. No one sets out with the intention to disregard their expert. Oftentimes it's driven by an abundance of passion and deep-seated knowledge of your organization and its operations. You know your business inside and out. That's your strength. But it can also become a blind spot when bringing in external expertise.

So how do you know if you're in danger of becoming a steam roller? Here are some questions to consider:

- When you bring someone on board does it still feel like it's solely your project, even though you've hired help?

- Do the people you hire seem to have little to add to the conversation or project development?

- Do you ever find that hiring an external agency or expert actually increases your workload rather than reducing it?

Answering 'yes' to any of these questions doesn't automatically make you a steam roller, but it's a signal that you may need to take a step back. If you find yourself nodding in agreement to more than one of these questions, it's worth considering that you might be stifling the expert's ability to deliver their best work.

Hiring an expert is about embracing their knowledge, skills, and fresh perspective. Yes, you are an expert in your business, and your input is essential. But remember, you've brought the expert in for their special expertise, so it's important to make space for them to shine. Be open to their ideas, encourage dialogue, and let them drive the aspects of the project that fall within their realm of expertise.

Navigating this dynamic is a delicate balance, but it's one that can lead to successful collaboration and project outcomes. So the next time you bring an expert into your organization, beware the steam roller. Recognize its signs, understand its impacts, and make the necessary adjustments to ensure you're enabling your expert to do what they do best, bringing their unique value to your project.

Banish Micromanaging

Micromanaging. A term that sends shudders down the spines of many. It's the act of controlling every part, however small, of an enterprise or activity. And it's a definite no-no when working with external experts. So let's talk about how we can banish micromanagement and make room for your expert's value to shine bright.

Steam rolling and micromanaging often go hand in hand. Both can stifle the creativity and capability of your expert, ultimately undermining the very reason you brought them on board. Creating an environment where your expert's skills and experiences can truly flourish is not just good manners; it's smart business.

When you're leading, or when your expert is part of a team of equal leaders, the way you structure results, assign tasks, and welcome expertise becomes critical. Carefully consider how you divvy up responsibilities. Assign tasks that play to each team member's strengths, and allow your expert to take the lead in areas where their knowledge outpaces that of the internal team.

Avoid the temptation to hover or nitpick over every detail. It's about trusting your expert's competence and their ability to deliver on the tasks at hand. Let them handle the intricacies of their assigned tasks, and keep the bigger picture in view. Your role here is to guide, not govern every step.

Intentionally creating space and inviting expertise is the key to leveraging the maximum value from experts. And that's really what it all boils down to. The more room your expert has to operate in their sphere of competence, the more value they bring to your organization.

Yes, loosening the reins can feel uncomfortable. Entrusting someone else, particularly an outsider, with important aspects of your organization might seem risky. But this leap of faith is necessary for growth and innovation. After all, experts are there to bring fresh perspectives and new ideas that your team might not have considered.

So banish micromanaging. Don't just hire experts, empower them. Encourage them to apply their expertise fully and freely. You've brought them in for their unique skills and experiences, so let them bring these to bear for the benefit of your project or organization. By doing this you ensure that you're not just hiring an expert but utilizing their full value. And that is a sure-fire recipe for success.

Clear Is Kind

Let's turn again to the wisdom of Brene Brown, who famously professed, "Clear is kind." This simple yet profound adage holds a wealth of value, particularly when it comes to expert engagements. Clarity is the cornerstone of a smooth, success-ful, and mutually beneficial collaboration. Let's break down the elements of clear communication and why it's so critical.

The importance of transparent, unambiguous communication cannot be overstated. Whether it's expressing project needs, of-fering feedback, or navigating hiccups along the way, maintain-ing clarity in all interactions is crucial.

This doesn't mean you have to be overly verbose or formal. Instead, ensure that your thoughts, ideas, and instructions are clearly conveyed and readily understandable. This minimizes chances for misunderstandings, improves efficiency, and fos-ters an open and respectful relationship between you and your expert. Yes, you've read it before and I'll say it again… com-municate early and often.

Here are some key areas to note for ensuring clarity in your communications:

Clear Expectations

Spell out what you anticipate from your expert, from the finer details of their role to the overall outcomes you aim to achieve. Be candid about what's within their purview and what's not, and about the level of autonomy they'll have. Remember, a well-briefed expert is a more efficient expert.

Clear Timelines

Alignment is key to successful collaborations. Specify deadlines for tasks and projects from the outset. Clear timelines not only help manage workflow but also ensure that everyone is on the same page about the project's progress and what needs to be done and when.

Specific and Detailed Agendas

When it comes to meetings, having a well-structured agenda can keep discussions on track, make time spent more valuable, and continuously propel the work forward. Agendas should clearly outline the key topics to be addressed, any preparatory work required, and the desired outcomes for the meeting.

Well-Defined Success

What does project success look like to you? A clear vision of a successful outcome is pivotal. Too many projects flounder because of nebulous end-goals. Defining what success looks like enables you to recognize when the objective has been met and also helps your expert understand exactly what they're working towards.

To wrap it up, clear is indeed kind. It paves the way for effective collaborations, reduces friction, and empowers your expert to deliver their best. Remember, clarity is not just about being understood. It's about making others feel seen, respected, and valued. So whenever you're working with an expert, make clarity your ally. It's not just kind; it's smart business, too.

Case Study: Navigating a Reality Check

This case study is a testament to the transformative power of having the right expert, especially when navigating the uncertain terrain of business growth. It explores the journey of a client operating a pet-focused business, with towering aspirations and the potential to scale, but who had a provider that wasn't delivering and was uncertain about the path to growth. This tale reveals the importance of having a process to hire the right expert and allowing the expert to lead in areas that feel uncertain.

The Situation

A thriving pet-focused brand was expanding its local service area and had ambitious plans for the future. However, a recent provider change for their local marketing efforts had stalled out leads and was taking growth plans off course.

The owner recognized something was wrong with the new provider, but didn't possess the expertise to diagnose or rectify the situation. On the operations side, the business was solid and primed for expansion. The ambition was there, but a clear strategy for growth was lacking. Questions about how to proceed and what steps to prioritize seemed daunting. Compounding this was the bigger vision of potentially franchising. They had the operational strength, but the roadmap for growth was unclear.

We met this client at an event where she started explaining her situation and we gave her some initial insights on ways to evaluate her provider and what kind of performance she could reasonably expect. From the conversation, she decided to hire us to correct the local marketing issue and chart a course for her to engage in growing her business.

The Plan

The first problem to solve was lack of leads. Looking into the existing provider's work, it was clear that the changes they had made reduced the company's visibility in search results. A plan was made to address that deficiency and metrics established to chart progress. In 3 months, the leads were back to the previous levels and other changes in the sales process had also increased the close rate.

Next up was to create a comprehensive strategy to formalize the company's position and blueprint for growth. This strategy would guide a brand update and inform a much-needed website overhaul. Our expertise was leveraged to map out a path that aligned with her goals and business vision.

Upon presenting our strategic plan, she was thrilled. She found that our team had not only understood but also truly captured her vision. We had effectively translated her aspirations into a clear, feasible strategy, outlining what she desired to build, her brand's unique value proposition, and its competitive edge in the saturated pet-focused market.

Getting to Work

Armed with this clear strategy, the first step was to define the updated brand. The world of branding and design can be a minefield, especially for founders. When every ounce of your passion, sweat, and tears has been poured into a business, it feels like an extension of you. It can be challenging to separate personal feelings from professional decisions when it comes to brand colors, taglines and logos.

The elevated brand concept we presented was a radical departure from the existing one. Factoring in the vision of a national brand, ready to franchise meant that the brand needed to be able to stand-out in relation to other national brands. Her initial reaction? Awe, excitement, even a touch of disbelief.

But as the novelty began to wear off and the sheer scale of the changes began to sink in, her initial excitement gave way to doubts. A tidal wave of realizations hit her—adopting the new brand meant changing everything associated with the current brand, from the website to marketing collateral and building signage. The costs, both financial and emotional, were overwhelming.

These newly considered factors caused her a bit of a "spin out" and she approached us with a laundry list of changes. Here's where the importance of hiring the right expert really matters. As her trusted advisor, our first task was to listen. Understand her concerns. Reassess her comfort levels. Figure out her motivations and what was behind all the change requests. Then, using that knowledge, to lead her through this challenge.

So we went back to the drawing board, reviewing our original project goals and checking whether the proposed path was indeed what she wanted. The gap between where she was and where she wanted to be seemed more of a chasm now. After re-evaluating the initial brand proposition and revisiting the project's core objectives, it became glaringly clear that she was not yet ready to take the big leap.

In helping clients achieve transformation, it's important to remember that it's not solely about delivering quality work. It's about tuning in to the client's needs and using strategy and planning to align our efforts with the intended results. Our job is not only to create and implement but also to guide and reassure.

In response to her apprehensions, we revisited the design and revised the logo and colors slightly. Instead of the original revolutionary update, we proposed an evolutionary progression of her existing brand, which was a significant step towards her grand vision but didn't require the giant leap she wasn't ready to make.

It would have been easier to cave to her list of requests, scrapping the initial proposal, and just churn out a variation of her existing brand. But that isn't the role of an expert. Our job was to partner with her, articulate her vision, and support her through this transformation, enabling her to serve her business' next phase. When it became apparent she wasn't prepared for a complete brand overhaul, we realigned the goalposts to match her comfort level and readiness. We recalibrated but we never lost sight of the bigger picture—the future success of her brand and business.

The Result

With the right expert, change can be dramatic and swift. Within just a few months of engaging with us, there was a significant difference in the trajectory of the business. The correction of the local marketing efforts led to an influx of leads, and the business—quite the underdog until then—found itself thriving.

With the clear strategy, updated brand and updated website there was a staggering 40% year-over-year growth, something that even the most optimistic of us hadn't predicted.

Lessons Learned

Every project has its unique set of challenges, and every client has their unique perspective. In this scenario, there were ample opportunities for things to go south. The client, feeling anxious about the magnitude of the changes we proposed, could have easily switched to steam roll mode, said no to everything, and fired us. But because we were partners in the project, kept communication open and committed to maintaining clarity about the project's strategy, we were able to work through the challenges.

A vital foundation for overcoming obstacles was having a clear understanding of her goals, her vision, and her target audience. We knew the 'who' and 'how' of her business—who she wanted to serve and how she intended to serve them. This foundational understanding was not only our North Star, guiding us through the project, but also a beacon for her when the need to shift the goalposts emerged.

Hiring the right expert isn't about having someone that can just deliver the project. It's about delivering it in a way that aligns with the client's vision, even when that vision undergoes a change midway.

And this leads us to another crucial lesson: flexibility. We often start out with a set of goals at the project's inception. But along the journey, when we are in the thick of the project, sometimes things may not feel quite right. At such times, it's crucial to pause, step back, and reassess. Are we still aligned with our original goals? Or have our understandings and aspirations evolved, requiring us to update our goals? Being able to do this without losing sight of the larger picture is an essential skill that every expert should possess.

Moreover, this case study underscores the significance of maintaining open and honest communication throughout the project. We kept the client in the loop and ensured she was on board with every decision. This open dialogue helped manage her apprehensions and keep us aligned with her vision, facilitating a win-win situation.

And it confirmed a belief we have about our work—that our job goes beyond just delivery. We are here to help articulate the client's vision, guide them through the transformation, and ensure the result serves their business in its next growth phase. When the going gets tough, we don't just capitulate. We reorient, realign, and march forward.

Chapter Nine
Detour

I'm reminded of a quote from the legendary boxer, Mike Tyson, who once mused, "Everyone has a plan until they get punched in the face." It's a sentiment that rings true in the boxing ring, life, and indeed the business world. Like a boxer we can train hard, create strategies, and envision our win, but sometimes the unexpected left hook can knock us off balance.

In the sphere of business, just as in life, perfection is a mirage. Even with the most diligent preparations, the choicest hires, and the most detailed planning, unexpected detours can and do occur. Your roadmap, no matter how meticulously charted, might need recalibration. In other words, as Tyson's quote implies, everyone has a plan, but those plans can get a real shakeup when faced with unforeseen challenges. And that's okay!

Engagements and projects are dynamic entities. They breathe, evolve, and sometimes deviate from their original path. That's not necessarily a bad thing. After all, growth often springs from places of discomfort and change. The key is to navigate these detours effectively, to pivot rather than faceplant. It's about being resilient, adaptable, and solutions-focused when things veer off course.

In this landscape of unpredictability, you might be wondering, is there a magic formula to guide us through? While there's no one-size-fits-all solution, there is indeed a standard formula that can serve as a beacon, leading us back onto the path when we drift. This formula, which we will explore further, isn't a cure-all, but rather a strategic approach to tackle challenges and put the project back on track.

There could be hundreds, if not thousands, of reasons why a project or engagement takes an unexpected detour. Every situation is different, each carrying its unique set of challenges. However, the application of the formula is universal. Regardless of the specific circumstances that led to the detour, this formula can provide much-needed clarity and direction.

In the upcoming sections, we will dive deep into various scenarios that might take you off course. For each situation we will explore how to apply our formula, dissect its workings, and illustrate how it can steer you back to your desired path. It's time to delve into the world of detours, navigational tools in hand, and discover the art of course-correction.

Follow These Signs

When navigating a project in turmoil, a tested and versatile compass is indispensable. Below is a step-by-step rescue map to guide you - a proven formula to salvage a project or engagement that has veered off course.

Moving from drowning confusion to smooth sailing involves crucial elements such as prioritizing in-person, real-time communication; acknowledging the issue and accepting your role in its occurrence; revisiting the original intent of the project; scrutinizing the standards of success established; re-establishing clear roles, particularly leadership and culminates in devising the blueprint to move forward. The not-so-secret way to effective salvage involves a willingness to embrace the uncomfortable, call out the elephant in the room and take action.

Recommended formula for salvaging a project or engagement:

1. **In-person, real-time communication.**

   When things go awry, it's essential to open up lines of real-time, in-person communication. Picking up the phone or setting a face-to-face meeting can bridge gaps that emails or texts might fail to cross. These immediate and personal communication channels create a platform for clear and open dialogue, paving the way for solutions.

2. **Identify and acknowledge the problem.**

   Pretending that everything is fine when it's not can only lead to more issues. Being upfront about the situation is a crucial step towards resolution. Admitting there's a problem might feel uncomfortable, but it can shed light on what's going wrong, fostering an environment for constructive conversations and effective problem-solving.

3. **Own your part: Take responsibility for whatever part you played.**

A misstep is a team effort, not the fault of an individual. Owning up to your contribution to the issue not only reflects personal integrity but also encourages others to do the same. Admitting your role in the hiccup can create an environment that values accountability, and opens the door for mutual understanding and reconciliation.

4. **Revisit the intent.**

It's essential to circle back to your original goals when things start going south. Aligning the team around the original intent or purpose of the project helps clear away any misunderstandings or miscommunications that might have led to the derailment. It acts as a beacon to guide everyone back onto the right track.

5. **Check in with the definition of success & update if needed.**

Remember the image of success you had when you started? Well, now is the time to bring it back into focus. Evaluate your original success metrics and see if they still hold. Change is the only constant, so don't hesitate to update your definition of success to align with new realities. This step ensures everyone is moving towards a common, updated goal.

6. **Re-establish roles, especially leadership.**

   In the midst of a detour, it's easy to forget who's steering the ship. Therefore, it's important to re-establish and reiterate roles, particularly the leadership ones. Everyone involved should know who's calling the shots, resolving disputes, and ensuring the project stays on track. This step reinforces a sense of order and direction, a beacon during the uncertainty of a project gone off course.

7. **Decide how to proceed.**

   The last piece of the puzzle is deciding on a solid plan to get things back on track. Often, the wisest approach is to have frequent check-ins or checkpoints. These act like regular pit-stops where you gauge progress, troubleshoot issues, and recalibrate direction if necessary. They serve as constant reminders of the path to the goal, keeping everyone aligned and accountable, ensuring that the project or engagement remains firmly on its path to success.

Now you have the steps, but information isn't valuable until you put it into action. Let's examine how you can apply these steps in a couple different "detour" scenarios you might encounter.

Detour Scenario #1: Expert Isn't Delivering

So, let's say you're dealing with an expert who just isn't delivering. Deadlines for deliverables have come and gone. Maybe they keep rescheduling meetings or even ghosting you. It can be a total pain, but don't panic. Setbacks are pretty much an inescapable part of the business world. And, we've got a roadmap - our handy seven-step formula after all:

Step 1: In-person, Real-time Communication

First, it's important to discuss the issue in person, or at least through a real-time method, like a video call. Email threads or chat messages can create confusion and lack the essential human elements—voice intonations, facial expressions, and body language. They help convey meaning and emotions that can be critical in such conversations. Hitch up your adulting britches (I get it, they aren't comfortable) and schedule a meeting as soon as possible to address the issue.

Step 2: Clearly Lay Out What Isn't Working

Next, clearly articulate what's not working. Being vague or overly diplomatic won't help. Is it the quality of the work? The timelines? The responsiveness? Pinpoint the issue precisely so it can be addressed head-on. Also, ensure you're being fair and basing your feedback on facts and not assumptions or emotions.

Put this clear articulation into an agenda for your issue on the meeting and determine what will show improvement or resolution for the issue(s). Be specific and make it measurable.

Step 3: Own Your Part

As a popular song lyric goes: Maybe you're the problem. Evaluate your role in the issue. It is possible you haven't been clear enough with your instructions. Or perhaps you haven't been available to provide the necessary guidance. Take ownership of any contribution you've made to the situation. It can help set the stage for a vulnerable conversation with your expert if you are courageous enough to open with ownership of any role you might have played in the issue.

Step 4: Revisit the Intent

Then, get back to basics. Revisit the original intent of the project. Discuss why you brought them on board in the first place, and what you both were hoping to achieve. Sometimes, revisiting the original vision can help both parties refocus and realign.

And sometimes, it becomes clear that they might not be able to deliver on the original intent, especially if there have been shifts in the organization or if additional complexities have been uncovered during the engagement. If that's the case, it might be time to talk about how to part ways (check out Part 3 for more on this).

Step 5: Check In with the Definition of Success & Update If Needed

Review the agreed-upon success criteria. If they're no longer realistic or relevant, it's time to update them. Be sure to involve the expert in this process in order to create a mutual understanding of what success looks like. You may even need to expand the definition of success to include previously unspoken expectations about deadlines or meetings.

Step 6: Re-Establish Roles, Especially Leadership

Are the roles still clear? Maybe the expert isn't delivering because they're unsure about some aspects of their role, or perhaps they're waiting on inputs they aren't getting. Clear these clouds. Reiterate your roles, the expert's roles, and anyone else who is involved.

Step 7: Decide How to Proceed

Finally, decide how to get back on track. Set up frequent check-ins to review progress, troubleshoot issues, and gauge whether the adjustments are working. These check-ins are especially crucial when a project is being course-corrected, and will help in closely monitoring the progress.

And there you have it. Troubles with expert deliveries can be quite a road bump, but with communication, clarity, accountability, and effective planning you can get your project back on track! Just stick to this seven-step formula and you're good to go.

Detour Scenario #2: Your Organization Isn't Responsive

Sometimes the expert is on point, but getting your organization to engage and participate is like a goat rodeo. This is certainly painful for you, and can be a soul-sucking experience for an expert trying to help you. Here's how the seven-step formula works in this scenario.

Step 1: In-Person, Real-Time Communication

Time to get in the room (physical or virtual) with all the internal stakeholders. This can be tough if the team is already busy, but it is critical. The agenda for the meeting will be to check in on the relative priority of the project with the expert. The key to success here is to convey your concerns empathetically, aiming for constructive dialogue, not finger-pointing. It is possible that the team has the best of intentions, they just have competing priorities

Step 2: Clearly Lay Out What Isn't Working

Clearly articulate where the responsiveness is lacking. Is it a delay in approvals, lack of feedback, or untimely communication? Cite specific instances if possible, so everyone understands the real impacts of these delays. The solution might be to change stakeholders or change stakeholder roles to ensure timely responses.

Step 3: Own Your Part

A bit different take on ownership here if the issue is with the internal team. Perhaps there haven't been clear expectations about turnaround times or there's a need to be more assertive about the project's priority or allotted time. A candid conversation here might reveal changes that can be made to how reviews are conducted or items provided that will make the participation of the team easier and more efficient.

Step 4: Revisit the Intent

Bring everyone back to the reason this project started in the first place. Remember the goals and objectives? Refresh everyone's memory and highlight how the lack of responsiveness is a roadblock to achieving these goals. This can reignite their commitment. This conversation may also reveal a shift in organizational priorities or resource allocations.

Step 5: Check In with the Definition of Success & Update If Needed

Review the success metrics of the project. Have they become unrealistic due to the lack of responsiveness? If yes, redefine the success criteria. Align them with the realities of your organization's communication culture while still pushing for better responsiveness.

Step 6: Re-establish Roles, Especially Leadership

Reconfirm everyone's roles and responsibilities in the project. Make sure to emphasize who is responsible for what and in what timeframe. Reinforce the leadership role, as it can often play a critical part in boosting responsiveness by setting the pace and tone.

Step 7: Decide How to Proceed

Finally, figure out the way forward. Set up regular checkpoints to monitor progress and check the improved responsiveness. Regular check-ins can help keep the project on track and ensure all parties stay engaged and committed.

So, that's it. Your organization's lack of responsiveness can be frustrating, but with open communication, clear expectations, and some degree of patience you can navigate your way through this hurdle and get your project back on track.

Detour Scenario #3: Too Many Cooks In the Kitchen

Ah, the old "too many cooks in the kitchen" scenario. Where everyone's got an opinion, and consensus feels like an impossible dream. This can be tricky, but the seven-step formula can help get you out of this jam, too. Here's how to apply it:

Step 1: In-Person, Real-Time Communication

First things first, gather all these creative (or not-so-creative) chefs in one place. Create a safe space where everyone can express their views without judgment. It's crucial to approach this meeting with an open mind and heart, and specific agenda.

Step 2: Clearly Lay Out What Isn't Working

Now, time for some honesty. Outline the issues that arise when everyone tries to lead. Draw attention to the confusion, delays, and inefficiencies it causes. This isn't about blaming but identifying the problems that need fixing. It could be that roles need more clear definition and possibly some kind of framework for resolving differing opinions (rock-paper-scissors is an option, but there are more sophisticated tie-breakers).

Step 3: Own Your Part

What's your part in this? Did you let too many people in on decision-making? Did you fail to set boundaries or clarify roles? Acknowledge your role in enabling the situation and be open to changes you need to make. Again, a little bit of vulnerability can go a long way, so it sometimes gets the room to open up if you start with owning your part.

Step 4: Revisit the Intent

Realign everyone to the project's original intent. Why are you all here? What are you trying to achieve? This common ground can act as a North Star, guiding everyone's decisions rather than personal biases or preferences. It can also help to un-invite opinions and hone-in on the desired business outcomes.

Step 5: Check In with the Definition of Success & Update If Needed

Review what success looks like for this project. Is it still attainable with the current chaos? If not, redefine success parameters in a way that's fair, realistic, and respects everyone's contributions but prevents decision-making paralysis.

Step 6: Re-Establish Roles, Especially Leadership

This is critical. Clearly define who's responsible for what. Who's the ultimate decision-maker? Who's advising? Who's executing? Be clear and firm about these roles in order to prevent overlapping responsibilities and decision-making bottlenecks.

Step 7: Decide How to Proceed

With everything laid out, decide the way forward. Incorporate regular check-ins to ensure everyone stays in their lanes and the project progresses smoothly. These check-ins can also act as avenues for everyone to provide their input without interfering with decision-making.

And voila! By applying these seven steps, you've turned a chaotic kitchen into a finely tuned, decision-making gourmet machine. But remember, it requires patience, persistence, and lots of communication. Keep the focus on your common goals, and you'll navigate your way out of this culinary nightmare.

Conclusion

You now have a better understanding of the nuances and dynamics involved in this kind of professional engagement. It's a journey that requires strategy, patience and, most importantly, a spirit of collaboration. Engagement with an expert is not just about hiring someone with the right skills. It's about forming a partnership, a collaboration where both parties are invested in achieving a common goal. It's about trust and respect, giving space, and being kind with clear communication.

The golden nuggets from this chapter boil down to a few key takeaways:

Establishing boundaries, setting clear expectations, and maintaining open lines of communication is critical when working with an expert. These factors serve as the bedrock of your partnership and can mean the difference between smooth sailing or a tumultuous journey.

Know your role and give experts the breathing room to do what they do best. Micromanaging can seem tempting when you're venturing into new territory, but it often serves to hinder the process rather than facilitate it. We've delved into the importance of creating space for the expert's skills and experience to shine. Allow your expert to take the wheel. You've hired them for their knowledge and expertise, so let them deliver their best work.

In our exploration of issues to avoid, we also uncovered the importance of **being clear**. Clear communication, clear expectations, clear timelines—these elements, although simple, are foundational to the success of any project. Being specific and detailed with agendas and having well-defined success criteria will help keep your project on track and moving forward.

The case study of a pet-focused brand brought these principles to life, illustrating the benefits of hiring the right expert. It highlighted the crucial role of the expert, who needs to listen, lead, and adapt based on the client's changing needs and circumstances. It also showed the power of being clear about the results you're after and using strategy and planning to guide your efforts. Even when things got sticky the ability to reset, realign, and keep marching forward proved invaluable.

The case study's successful outcome wasn't just due to hiring the right expert. It was a direct result of open communication, setting clear expectations, allowing the expert space to work, and being adaptable and flexible in the face of change.

When working with experts consider them as an extension of your team. Listen to their advice, learn from their experience, trust their expertise and, most importantly, value their contribution. Doing so will not only help you make the most out of the engagement but also help your business or project to grow and prosper.

These principles can serve as your compass, guiding you towards a successful and fulfilling engagement with your chosen experts.

PART III
The Big Finish

And now the final section of the journey. This concluding part will guide you through the crucial steps to wrap up an expert engagement effectively and retain the maximum value from it. Let's embrace the end just as we embraced the start, with attentiveness and intentionality.

The first chapter addresses the essential closure actions. Here, we'll delve into the importance of a Project Close Checklist and discuss the best practices for offboarding an expert. This phase is vital as it ensures a seamless and beneficial conclusion for everyone involved.

Following is the chapter on "Handling an Unexpected End to an Expert Relationship." Not all projects go according to plan; some require a premature halt. We'll explore how to navigate these tough situations, the process of "Breaking Up," and deciding when "Firing Is the Right Choice." We also include some "Stories of Parting Ways."

Finish strong with the final chapter, "Tools to Make Ending a Relationship with an Expert Easier." We emphasize the significance of offboarding and share some potent tools and strategies to make this process smoother.

This section provides a comprehensive roadmap to tying up loose ends professionally and maximizing the return from your expert engagement.

Chapter Ten
When the Project Ends, How to Ensure a Smooth Hand-off

Happy Dance! You've found your golden-goose expert, and together you've navigated through the trials and triumphs of your project. They brought their A-game, and you've seen real, tangible improvements. Now, as the final project checkpoint looms on the horizon, you might be wondering, "What's next?" There's an echo of, "Is this where we part ways?" in the back of your mind.

Trust me, you're not alone in this. The conclusion of a project often stirs a mix of emotions—relief, satisfaction, and even a touch of nostalgia. And while it's great to revel in the sense of accomplishment, it's essential not to overlook the practical aspects. The end of a project doesn't necessarily mean the end of responsibilities or considerations.

There's a specific art to concluding a project. Often, the final meeting and handoff is seen as the last hurdle. You exchange congratulations, discuss the results, and then...it's done. But what if it isn't? What if there's a loose end, a lingering question, or an unanticipated problem that crops up post-project?

Let's go back to why you hired an expert in the first place. You sought their assistance to achieve growth, improve a specific area, or add capacity to your organization. The ultimate goal wasn't just to wrap up the project, but to create lasting value that would continue to benefit your organization even after the engagement ended. This is where the hand-off becomes paramount. It's not just about wrapping up the current project, but effectively bridging to the next phase of utilizing the value that's been created.

A smooth hand-off is like passing the baton in a relay race. It requires clear communication, understanding, and precision. The expert you hired has spent significant time and effort to create an asset, a solution, a result. Now, it's time to ensure that this asset can be effectively leveraged by your team.

Here's a little nugget of wisdom: experts are not just for the duration of the project, but are resources for guidance throughout the process and even after. As a client, it's your job to think about what lies beyond the project's end. Are there maintenance tasks your team needs to take on? What's the best way to utilize and capitalize on the work that's been done? And how do you ensure that the transition is as smooth as silk?

As you're wrapping up the project, it's wise to have an exit or disengagement strategy in place. This isn't a sign of anticipating failure; instead, it's a sign of thorough planning. You've put so much effort into ensuring a successful engagement that it only makes sense to ensure a successful disengagement, too. A disengagement procedure can help make the transition smoother and ensure that you're set up for continued success even after the expert has stepped back.

Remember, maximizing the success of your expert engagement isn't confined to the project's active phase alone. It extends beyond, into the project's conclusion, and how well you prepare for the subsequent tasks. So as you approach the end of the project, keep these considerations in mind to ensure a seamless hand-off and a successful transition to the next phase of your journey. It's not just about ending well, but about launching into the next chapter effectively and efficiently.

Project Close Checklist

A smooth project wrap-up can make a world of difference. It's like the satisfying click of a puzzle piece slotting into place. That final moment when you can step back, appreciate the big picture, and confirm, "Yep, we've nailed it!"

To reach that satisfying conclusion, you'll want a nifty little guide. Let's call it our 'Project Close Checklist'. This checklist is the roadmap to ensuring your project doesn't just end with a bang but also sets you up for continued success. You see, a project's end isn't just about putting a check in the 'Done' box; it's about setting the stage for what comes next. With a good hand-off, you can continue to build on the great work that's been done, capitalizing on your investment and efforts.

Now, hold your horses before you start racing through this checklist! There's a little caveat you need to be aware of. In the world of business and engagements, not everything might be included in the project's original scope. Sometimes, certain steps or considerations may not have been a part of the original game plan. And that's okay! The key is to communicate, be aware, and adapt.

You're probably thinking, "Got it, but how do I navigate this?" Simple. Have a chat with your expert. Discuss this checklist, explore what's included in the project's scope, and be aware of what might require a separate conversation. Transparency and open communication are your allies in this journey, ensuring that nothing falls through the cracks or springs up as a surprise.

By proactively addressing these details, you're not just ticking off tasks; you're setting your project up for a successful closure and even more successful future utilization.

So here's your checklist:

- **Ask the expert how it wraps up.** This might seem obvious, but you'd be surprised how many people skip this vital step. Who better to ask about project wrap-up than the expert you've been working with, right? These professionals have likely done this dance more times than they can count, so they're familiar with the steps. They might have a clear roadmap to project closure, or they might need a nudge. Either way, kick off your conversation by asking how they typically wrap things up. They might just offer insights you hadn't thought of.

- **Figure out what you need to be successful post-project.** Every organization has its own rhythm, its unique way of doing things. Your team is no different. You've got those special quirks, particular habits that make you...well, you! Recognizing these unique aspects is key to figuring out what you need to successfully carry the baton post-project. Maybe it's weekly team meetings to revisit progress, perhaps it's a shared cloud space where everyone can access project-related files. Whatever it is, map it out. Ensure you've got everything you need to make the most of what you're handed.

- **Documentation.** The good ol' hand-off document. It's a staple in any project wrap-up process. It could be a user guide, project reference, or detailed documentation. Find out what your expert will provide. But here's the twist: don't just accept what's given. Take a moment to think about how your organization will use this info. Does the documentation align with your needs? Does it need to be modified, simplified, expanded? It could be as simple as determining who's going to be the keeper of this information. Make sure the documentation serves you, not the other way around.

- **Will you need more help?** This is the moment of truth. The project is ending, but does the work really stop? Perhaps there are ongoing tasks related to the project. Maybe there's a new need that's come to light. Be honest with yourself. If you need additional help, ask for it. Your expert should have this in their wrap-up agenda, but in case they don't, bring it up.

This checklist is a tool for ensuring the end of the project isn't a full-stop, but rather a bridge to future success. Be inquisitive, proactive, and most importantly, be ready to take full advantage of the value your expert engagement has created.

One of the best ways to extend this victory lap into the following weeks is to give yourself at least a solid 10-minute breather to walk through our handy-dandy checklist. Trust me, taking this small slice of time now can save you a whole lot of "Oh snap, we forgot about this" moments later.

Now, don't just run through the checklist, schedule that all-important wrap-up and hand-off meeting. It's like your project's final hoorah. Here you'll be dotting the I's and crossing the T's, making sure no loose ends remain untied. Think of it like the cherry on top of your project sundae. It's the final, integral part that leaves everyone feeling satisfied.

And yes, a successful conclusion might take a couple of hours in total. But look at it this way: it's the final act, the grand finale of your expert engagement. By investing this time now, you're ensuring that your project doesn't just end, but concludes successfully, with everything neatly packaged, documented, and understood by all.

So as you're basking in that warm glow of achievement, don't forget to put a bow on it. Tie everything off neatly, ensure everyone's on the same page, and then take a moment to pat yourself on the back. You've navigated an expert engagement, seen a project through to its end, and made sure it's set to continue delivering value.

Offboarding Your Expert

You know that sad, yet satisfying moment at the end of a great movie, where the plot line has resolved and the credits start rolling? That's kind of what it feels like when you're wrapping up a successful project with your expert. Except, instead of movie credits, you're navigating through the offboarding process. Sounds fun, right? I promise, it's not as daunting as it might seem.

In this section, we're diving into the nitty-gritty of saying 'see ya later' to your expert. No, it's not about sending them a farewell fruit basket (though, that's not a bad idea). We're talking about orchestrating the last dance, the final act, the close of the show—offboarding your expert in a way that keeps everyone smiling and everything seamless.

We'll be guiding you through your final meeting, where you'll wrap up all the loose ends, discuss the fantastic journey you've taken together, and plan for the future. We'll walk you through how to handle the transition of access to assets—because, let's face it, that's a shared responsibility between you and your expert.

We'll also discuss software and account access, because the last thing you want is to suddenly realize your expert still has the keys to the kingdom. And finally, what about those lingering questions that pop up after your expert has left the building? We've got you covered.

Final Meeting

The final meeting with your expert is a pivotal step in transitioning the project's reins back to your team. The agenda and duration of this meeting are vital to ensure it hits all the right notes and leaves no loose ends.

Let's start by talking about the duration. If you're thinking, "Oh, I'll just schedule a quick 30-minute meeting, how long can it really take?" pause right there. This isn't a stand-up meeting where you're updating the status of ongoing tasks. This is more akin to a project post-mortem or a strategy session. So, realistically, you should block out a good 60-90 minutes for this conversation. You want enough time to delve into the depth of what's been accomplished, discuss any final deliverables, and plan next steps without feeling rushed. You can also do two 45-minute meetings, as you might need some time between meetings to chase down any loose ends.

So, what should be on the agenda for this meeting? Here's a suggested rundown:

1. **Recap the journey.** Start with a bit of nostalgia. Recap the

project journey, highlighting key accomplishments and challenges overcome. This sets a positive tone and reminds everyone about the value generated by the engagement.

2. **Review final deliverables.** Walk through the final deliverables. Make sure you understand everything that's been handed over to you and your team, and clarify any questions you have about it. You don't want to discover a week later that you have no idea how to interpret that critical report your expert left you with.

3. **Discuss future responsibilities.** Clearly understand what responsibilities your team is taking on once the expert steps back. Whether it's managing a newly set-up process, maintaining a piece of software, or interpreting data from a newly implemented analytics system, make sure you know who is responsible for what.

4. **Plan for potential follow-up.** Agree on how any follow-up questions will be handled. You might not have everything perfectly lined up in your mind just yet. You want to be able to reach out to your expert with queries that might surface later.

5. **Feedback exchange.** Provide feedback to your expert about the engagement, and invite them to share their feedback as well. This will help both sides grow and learn from the experience.

6. **Celebrate success.** Finally, take a moment to celebrate your joint success. Appreciate the journey you've taken together,

and acknowledge the hard work put in by both sides.

The final meeting is your moment to ensure everything is well-understood, responsibilities are clear, and to set the stage for a successful hand-off.

Handling Access to Assets: Shared Responsibility Between You and the Expert

As the project winds down, another important part of the off-boarding process is managing access to assets. This is like the carefully orchestrated exchange of keys when you sell a car or house, or end a lease. However, in this digital age, keys don't just open doors; they also open files, databases, email accounts, and even proprietary software.

The handling of access to assets should be a shared responsibility between you and the expert. It needs to be executed with clear communication and respect for both parties' roles.

First, establish a comprehensive list of all the digital assets and physical resources your expert had access to during the project. From databases and software to office spaces and equipment, this list will act as your checklist. For each item, determine whether access should be maintained, limited, or removed completely.

Where things get a bit tricky is when the assets in question are projects or tasks that your expert was working on and might still be in progress. You'll want to arrange a 'soft' handover for these assets. Have your expert take you through each task, explaining the work done so far, any pending issues, and what needs to be done next. This isn't a game of hot potato; you want a smooth transition that doesn't disrupt your operations.

With digital assets, it's crucial to handle this process deliberately to avoid data loss or disruption to your systems. For shared files or documents, make sure they're transferred to a team member's ownership or a general company account. For software access, consult with your IT department or a trusted tech-savvy colleague to ensure a smooth and secure transition.

The same care should be taken with physical assets. Any equipment, keys, or access cards should be returned and accounted for. While this may seem old-school, failing to address this can lead to unexpected headaches down the road.

Last, let's not forget about confidential information. Your expert may have had access to sensitive data about your business, clients, or employees during their engagement. It's vital to have an agreement in place regarding the handling of this information post-engagement.

Remember, while offboarding your expert it's not about slamming doors shut. It's more about easing them gently closed, making sure that nothing valuable gets jammed in the process. You've invested time and money into this project, so the way you handle the endgame can greatly influence the long-term value you derive from it.

Software and Account Access

Now that we've covered handling access to physical and digital assets in general, let's zero in on a particularly sensitive area of software and account access. This aspect of offboarding your expert can be a tad complex, depending on the scale of your project and the various systems your expert had been given the keys to. Here's how to handle it with tact, grace, and a good dose of digital know-how.

Software access involves all those nifty applications and platforms your expert was using to do their job. This might range from task management systems like Asana or Jira, to complex databases or even cloud-based storage like Google Drive or Dropbox. Now, you don't want to be hasty and simply boot the expert out of all these systems the moment the clock strikes project end. That's a bit like yanking the tablecloth out from under a fully set table—it could be a mess.

Instead, work with your expert to identify all the systems they've used, and what information or work resides in each. Where the work is complete and there's no longer a need for access, go ahead and remove their permissions, ideally with the expert present, just to ensure no necessary data goes missing in the process.

However, with ongoing tasks or projects, or in instances where the expert's insights may still be needed for a period post-project, consider limiting their access instead. This could mean changing their permissions to 'view only' or similar. It's a case of putting up the glass cases, while still allowing them to browse the exhibit.

At the end of the day, it's crucial to ensure that control over all software and accounts resides firmly with the client—that's you. This means not just having admin access, but understanding what's in there. Your expert can help with this by providing a guided tour of the software and the work they've completed.

Remember, this process can be systematic, careful, and collaborative. It's about preserving and taking control of the work done, not just about locking the expert out. Be sure to discuss this step in detail with your expert. Some might even have their own offboarding process for this.

Overall, dealing with software and account access is a bit like cleaning up after a party. You want to make sure all guests have left, turn off the music, take out the trash, and then finally, lock the doors. In doing so, you're not just ending the party, you're also setting the stage for a fresh start the next day.

Questions Afterwards

Alright, so you've had your final meeting, sorted out access to assets, and tidied up all the software and account access details. Job done, right? Well, almost. There's just one more crucial aspect of offboarding your expert to consider: what happens when you have questions afterwards? And trust me, you probably will, because let's face it, nobody knows your project like the expert you just worked with. So, how should you go about this?

First off, let's start with this: don't be shy. When questions pop up after the project has officially ended, don't hesitate to reach out to your expert. Most professionals understand that queries may arise once the dust has settled and are often willing to help provide clarity. Remember, your success reflects on them, so it's in their best interest to ensure you're confidently carrying forward the work they've done.

But here's the key: respect boundaries. Understand that once the project wraps up, your expert's commitment to you has technically ended. They might be engrossed in new projects and might not have the capacity to respond immediately. So treat this as a favor, not an obligation. Be patient and appreciative of their time.

Before the project ends, it's a great idea to discuss this possibility with your expert. Establish a protocol for post-project communications. Some experts may include a certain amount of post-project support in their fees, while others may charge extra. Clear this up to avoid surprises down the line.

You can even plan for the inevitable by asking the expert to prepare a 'knowledge base' or a 'frequently asked questions' guide related to the project. This can act as your first line of defense when questions pop up, and it'll reduce the need for back-and-forth emails or calls.

In the end, offboarding isn't just about bringing the project to a close. It's about setting you up for success as you continue on your journey. So, when you have questions afterwards—and it's almost certain you will—don't fret. Reach out, ask for the help you need, and keep on building upon the great work you and your expert accomplished together.

Chapter Eleven
Tools to Make Ending a Relationship with an Expert Easier

B reakups. We've all been there, right? Whether it's with a romantic partner, a longtime pal, or even a business relationship, they can be tricky. While you haven't actually left your lucky socks in their drawer, maybe you did leave your coveted client files on their shared drive, or that essential access password in their inbox. Awkward? You bet.

That's why we're going to take a look at how we can use a blend of technology, tools, and savvy processes to ensure ending an expert relationship is less "Please, can I have my favorite hoodie back?" and more "Thanks for the memories, let's wrap this up cleanly."

Think of this as your personal guide to breakups, business-style. We're not dealing with broken hearts here; we're talking about ending expert relationships with grace, respect, and minimum fuss. It's all about making sure you take all your stuff with you when you walk out the door, leaving no loose ends and no reason for awkward calls when something comes up missing later.

In essence, this chapter is all about creating a smooth exit strategy. It's about how to untangle your business affairs from an expert relationship without feeling like you've been through an emotional wringer. By the time we're done you'll be well-equipped to handle the end of an expert relationship with all the finesse of a seasoned pro.

Offboarding Is as Important as Onboarding

Offboarding often plays second fiddle to its more glamorous sibling, onboarding. I mean, let's face it, beginnings are just more exciting, aren't they? We're eager to make that perfect first impression, show off our skills, and get the ball rolling. We invest so much in the onboarding process—all the effort, the prep work, the grand plans—all aimed at launching that relationship on the best possible footing. But what about when it's time to say goodbye?

In a perfect world, we would have a flawless offboarding process for every project, ready to implement when the time comes. Yet, in reality, it's often an afterthought. It gets tossed aside, neglected like the last potato chip in a bag that's slightly too burnt to be enjoyed. But this 'burnt chip', this overlooked area, actually deserves center stage. Offboarding is vital and can help ensure a clean, efficient, and above all, amicable closure to an expert relationship.

When we're caught up in the excitement of a new project, the thought of how it might end is often the furthest thing from our minds. But ignoring the offboarding process during onboarding can set you up for a whirlwind of confusion when the relationship ultimately draws to a close.

As the client, it's in your best interest to extract the maximum value from your expert relationships. This isn't limited to just the work you receive but extends to the overall management and completion of the relationship. By implementing your own systems and encouraging your experts to work within these frameworks, you can drive efficiency, increase productivity, and maintain a healthy working relationship.

That being said, it's equally important to keep some key areas in mind when wrapping up an expert relationship. Like an experienced chef mindful of every ingredient, these 'ingredients' of the offboarding process will ensure you're left with a palatable result, not a burnt-out mess. After all, ending a relationship doesn't have to feel like cleaning up after a tornado has just swept through your project. With the right systems and processes, you can ensure a smooth exit that leaves both parties satisfied and ready for their next adventure.

A Management System

When the curtain comes down on an expert relationship, it can feel a bit like cleaning up after a great party. The memories are great, the results were worth it, but now there's a certain level of let's say, 'mess', to deal with. The trick to avoiding this clean-up operation is a bit of forethought and the clever use of a management system.

First things first, what's a management system? Picture a tool kit. A management system is a bit like that, but for your business. It's a collection of policies, processes, and procedures that help an organization fulfill its objectives. These objectives can be as diverse as ensuring customer requirements are met, complying with regulations, or even meeting environmental targets.

But here's the catch, this isn't a one-size-fits-all kind of deal. Each management system is tailored to a specific area of an organization's operation, focusing on those particular requirements. However, all systems share some common elements, like leadership commitment, risk assessment, objective setting, process identification, monitoring, measurement, and continual improvement.

Now, you might be thinking, "Great, another system to learn." But hold your horses. The beauty of a management system is that it should integrate with your internal processes. It's not about reinventing the wheel; it's about adding some turbo boosters.

Let's use our agency as an example. We use Google Workspace. It's a one-stop-shop that connects our team, creating a flow of information that everyone can dip into. It's the digital equivalent of having all your documents in one big, perfectly organized, searchable filing cabinet (that also happens to have built-in collaboration and communication tools).

But remember, this isn't about the software; it's about the method. Other agencies might use Microsoft Office 365, Zoho, or another platform. The key here is to ensure you're getting the most out of whatever system you're using. Just like a well-oiled machine, your management system needs to run smoothly, integrating with your day-to-day processes and enhancing your productivity.

Sure, it might take a little elbow grease to get it up and running, but once you're in the groove, a good management system can work wonders. It ensures that even after an expert has finished their work, you've got everything you need in a neat, easy-to-find package. No hunting for lost files, no confusion over who did what, and no awkward emails asking for that one document you just can't find.

By investing some time into setting up a robust management system, you're investing in peace of mind. It's like hiring an ultra-efficient personal assistant to keep track of everything. When it's time to wrap up a project, you'll have everything at your fingertips, saving you time, reducing stress, and keeping your operations running smoothly.

A Repository or User Guide

Just like how every bestseller has a table of contents, your collaboration with an expert should have one, too. It's not just about having all the relevant documents, assets, and processes in one place. It's also about making sure they're easy to find and easy to understand. That's where a repository or user guide comes in.

Let's paint a picture. Imagine a new client. There's a certain level of excitement and energy buzzing in the air. We like to harness this energy right from the get-go. We begin by creating a dedicated Google Drive folder for them. Think of it as their personal workspace in our digital world.

As we navigate the journey together, we also start building a user guide. The user guide is our compass, a crucial tool that evolves with our collaboration. It's a dynamic Google Doc that contains links to everything necessary for the project.

From specific processes to important documents, from treasured assets to those little nuggets of information that keep the project running smoothly, the user guide is the ultimate cheat sheet for our team. It's the single source of truth, the first point of reference when someone needs to dig up information about the client's project.

As the client relationship evolves the user guide becomes richer, filled with a wealth of information, becoming a virtual treasure chest of insights and resources.

But why do we do this? Well, because goodbyes are inevitable. And when that day comes, we want to ensure a smooth transition. By handing over this comprehensive document, we make sure our clients have everything they need in one place.

Whether they choose to continue the work themselves or engage with another provider, they have a head start.

The user guide, paired with the repository (Google Drive folder in our case), ensures that all the puzzle pieces are in one place, complete with a map to use them effectively.

Of course, this doesn't mean you need to use Google. If you're more of a Microsoft 365 person, you might opt for a OneDrive folder and a Word doc. Or, if Dropbox is your jam, a Dropbox Paper document and a Dropbox folder might be the way to go.

The point is, it's not about the platform you use; it's about having a single, easily accessible location where all resources are stored. Alongside it, there should be a guide detailing what's stored and how to access it. This might include links to items not necessarily stored in the folder, like Canva templates, videos, analytics documents, reports, or any other relevant material.

In essence, this dynamic duo of a repository and user guide becomes your project's bible. It's a tool that offers a blend of ease, organization, and accessibility, ensuring you have a smooth offboarding process. It's the go-to place that holds your project's past, present, and future. So even when the expert relationship concludes, the journey can continue without a hitch.

Chapter Twelve
Handling an Unexpected End to an Expert Relationship

L et's face it, not every story ends with a happily-ever-after. You've put in your best efforts, but there are times when life (or business) throws you a curveball. The road can sometimes get bumpy, and there might be a need for an unexpected exit. This is equally true in the world of business relationships, particularly when it comes to those between a client and an expert.

In the previous chapters, we laid out a road map to conclude a project smoothly with an expert, a sort of guide to a clean and pleasant parting. However, the reality is that every situation doesn't always afford us the luxury of a neat conclusion. Changes come in many forms. Maybe someone lands a new role, or a company is caught in the whirlwind of mergers and acquisitions, or sometimes the expert just isn't cutting it anymore.

So here we are, about to dive into the rough waters of unexpected endings. Yes, it's an uncomfortable topic, but it's essential. Let's think of it this way: Knowing how to handle a tricky situation like this is as important as knowing how to foster a successful relationship.

In this chapter, we're lifting the lid on the less-than-pleasant, yet sometimes necessary, process of unexpectedly ending a client-expert relationship.

Breaking Up Is Hard to Do

Breaking up is hard to do. Sounds like the title of a sad song, doesn't it? We've all been there in some shape or form. Whether it's a personal relationship or a professional one, breakups are just...ugh. They're packed with a whole mess of emotions, awkward conversations, and those classic "It's not you; it's me" lines that are really just a polite way of saying, "No, it's definitely you."

And let's be honest. When you're in a relationship that has run its course, whether it's with an expert or a significant other, it's no picnic to be the one who has to stand up and call it quits. It's a weird cocktail of guilt and relief, especially if you suspect the other party is just as keen to split.

This discomfort often leads us to prolong relationships that should have ended ages ago. We delude ourselves into thinking that if we just wait it out, the situation will somehow resolve itself without us having to lift a finger. It's a bit like a magical thinking exercise, where you hope for a turn of events that will spare you from being the bad guy. I remember going through this exact situation with a college boyfriend. I was convinced he'd graduate and move away so I wouldn't have to do the breaking up. Well, he graduated alright, but guess who didn't move away? You got it, I had to be the one to pull the plug (and, just to spice things up, he ended up becoming my sister's brother-in-law, so that wasn't awkward at all).

From someone who has been there, done that: Waiting it out is almost always worse than just biting the bullet and dealing with the issue head-on.

Now, I'm not saying that you need to channel your inner reality TV show host and shout, "You're fired!" across a boardroom table. In fact, don't do that, please. There's no need to make the situation more dramatic than it needs to be.

The key is to approach the situation with empathy and understanding. It's about raising issues in a respectful way and understanding that ending a relationship that's not working is ultimately better for everyone involved.

When a relationship comes to an end, it's not about assigning blame. It's about acknowledging that the dynamics of the relationship are no longer serving the purpose they were meant to. It's recognizing that the project or the work or the collaboration is not progressing as it should, and making the tough decision to change course.

It's about doing what's best for your organization, your team and, yes, even the expert. Sometimes that means ending the relationship and finding a new path forward.

The upside of all this? You grow. You learn. You get better at navigating these choppy waters. And the more you do it, the easier it gets to recognize when a relationship is no longer working and to act accordingly.

So, yes, breaking up is hard to do, but sometimes it's the right thing to do. It's an uncomfortable conversation, sure, but it's also an opportunity for growth—for both you and the expert.

Sometimes, Firing Is the Right Choice

When you're in the business world you're always striving to grow, improve, and increase capacity. That's why we bring experts or external agencies into the fold—to provide that extra oomph to help us reach our goals. It's a little bit like adding a turbocharger to your engine. But here's the thing about growth... it rarely happens in a straight line. We all evolve and change, and that includes both the business and the expert.

In an ideal world, the evolution of the business and the expert are perfectly synchronized. They grow in the same direction, at similar rates, like synchronized swimmers performing a flawless routine. But let's be real, we don't live in an ideal world. Sometimes the business and the expert grow at different paces, or in completely different directions. Imagine our synchronized swimmers suddenly deciding to do freestyle and butterfly strokes instead. Not quite as harmonious, right?

This divergence can happen for any number of reasons. Maybe you discover that the expert isn't quite the right fit for your company. Like when you buy a pair of shoes that looks great in the store, but when you take them home they pinch your toes and make you walk like you've got a pebble in your shoe. Or perhaps the players in the game change. People in key roles leave or are replaced, and the dynamics of the relationship shift. It's like changing the lead singer of a band—the tunes just aren't the same anymore.

There could also be situations where there's simply a lack of performance or results. Like hiring a personal trainer to get in shape, but all you're losing is time and money, not weight. In such cases, it's clear that something isn't working.

Life is in a constant state of flux, and that's as true in business as it is in nature. In other words, "shift happens." And when shift happens, you can't just brush it under the rug and pretend everything's fine. That's like trying to fix a leaky faucet with duct tape. It might hold for a while, but it's not a permanent solution.

So when this sort of shift happens, it's crucial to address it head-on. That might mean having a heart-to-heart with your expert, redefining roles, or even ending the relationship entirely. Yes, firing someone. As tough as it may sound, sometimes firing is the right choice.

It doesn't mean you've failed or that the expert is terrible. It's simply a recognition that the current arrangement isn't serving its purpose anymore. It's a tough call to make, and making the tough calls is part of the job. So when shift happens, roll up your sleeves, address it, and remember that sometimes firing is the right choice.

The Breakup

Okay, let's get down to the nitty-gritty, folks. We've all been there, haven't we? You're sitting on a powder keg of issues, silently praying that everything will miraculously sort itself out, but deep down you know the shift is about to hit the fan. And let me tell you, once that mess gets airborne it's even harder to sit down and have that crucial conversation in your client-expert relationship. By that time the ship may have already sailed, the goose is nearly cooked, the relationship might just be too far gone to salvage.

So how do you navigate this sticky situation? How do you tell the other party, "It's time to pack up and hit the road, Jack," but with an air of professionalism and tact? Well, stick around because we're about to break it down into a step-by-step guide that'll make even the toughest breakups feel like a walk in the park.

Communicate Early & Often

As you've heard me say before, communication is the bread and butter of any successful relationship. Whether it's your partner, your kids, your best friend, or in this case your expert, one thing remains crystal clear: you've got to communicate, and you've got to do it early and often.

I remember attending a seminar where a speaker threw a question at us: "What's the leading cause of divorce?" From all corners of the room, the familiar answers rang out: lies, infidelity, money troubles. But surprise, surprise, the true answer is... drumroll, please... unmet expectations! Yep, you heard it right. Not the steamy affairs or sneaky lies, but simply expectations that were set but never fulfilled.

Now, you may be wondering, "What does divorce have to do with my expert-client relationship?" Stick with me here. You see, just like in a marriage, the relationship with your expert is a two-way street. It's an ongoing dialogue, a dynamic exchange, not a one-sided monologue. You both have expectations, goals, and requirements. If these aren't met or, worse, not communicated at all, then you're setting up a breeding ground for disappointment and frustration.

Ideally, you'd have a system in place, a regular checkpoint where you can air out concerns, rectify small hiccups before they become overwhelming roadblocks, and generally stay in tune with the status of the relationship. And by relationship, I don't mean whether you're ready to invite them to your annual summer barbecue. No, I'm talking about the work, the projects, the output. Is it going well, or does it feel like you're trying to paddle upstream?

But here's the catch: Not every relationship has this setup, this open channel of communication. If you find yourself in this boat, it's time to put on your big-person pants and be the one to break the ice. Speak up, air those concerns, voice the issues, because you know what? That silence isn't golden; it's downright harmful. So, for the love of all that is good, communicate!

Own Your Part

Alright, let's talk about accountability, and no I'm not about to give you a lecture on accountability. But here's the truth, and it's as straightforward as it gets: every relationship is a dance, and it takes two to tango. You might've hired an expert, but this dance isn't a solo show. You're both on the dance floor, so it's only fair to own up to your steps (even the missteps).

Why is this important? Because acknowledging your part in the situation isn't just about pointing fingers or playing the blame game. It's about reflecting on your actions, decisions, and maybe even omissions that may have contributed to the current situation. And trust me, this self-reflection is as valuable as gold.

Sometimes just being honest with yourself and recognizing your own shortcomings can lead to solutions you hadn't considered before. You might just find that the seemingly insurmountable problem has a solution within your reach, a tweak in your own systems and processes, or a change in the way you communicate or delegate tasks.

And even if it doesn't magically fix the problem (because, let's face it, life's not a fairy tale), owning your part will make you wiser, and better equipped for the future. It'll help you understand what you could've done differently, what to look out for, how to set clearer expectations, or how to choose your next expert.

After all, every bump on the road is an opportunity to learn and grow. So don't shy away from owning your part, however uncomfortable it might be. You might be surprised at the potential growth that lies hidden in this acknowledgment.

Clearly Identify What You Want to Have Happen Next

Now, this sounds like something out of a self-help book, but hey, aren't we all looking for a little guidance? If you're the client and the expert or agency you hired has bobbled, bungled, or just plain botched something, it's on you to figure out where to go from there.

And no, I don't mean you have to fix their mess. But you do have to decide what you want as a next step. Are you looking for them to rectify the issue? Or have you reached a point where you just want to cut your losses and end the relationship?

The thing is, you can't expect them to read your mind any more than you can read theirs (unless you've got some kind of psychic abilities you've been holding out on us, and if so, cool).

So be clear, be direct, and articulate what you want to happen next.

Whether it's a matter of "Hey, you messed this up, here's what I need you to do to fix it," or a "This isn't working out, here's how we're going to wrap things up," make sure you're leading the conversation towards a resolution that works for you. Remember, clarity is the key here.

Agree on the Separation Plan

The separation plan is a roadmap that outlines how you'll untangle your professional lives. It's not just about saying adios and slamming the door on your way out (tempting as that might be). Nope, it's about having an open and frank discussion about how you'll both navigate the waters of uncoupling in the professional sense.

Much like a divorce settlement (did I just make this awkward?), it's a place where unspoken expectations can cause an avalanche of misunderstandings, resentments, and those dreaded one-star Google reviews. You're not looking to air your dirty laundry in public. You're aiming for a professional, amicable separation (even if you are cursing them in your head).

As the client, you need to be clear on your expectations about how this relationship should end. No hinting, no vague implications. Spell it out. Need them to wrap up certain tasks? Say so. Want all passwords handed over? State it. Need them to train a replacement? Be explicit.

Remember, your expert or agency might have access to files, data, systems, or information that's crucial to your business. Or they might be in the middle of tasks you're not aware of. So make sure you ask what's needed from them to make the separation as smooth as possible.

Your goal here isn't to burn bridges, but to build a sturdy one you both can cross towards your separate futures. So, breathe deep, strap on your big-kid boots, and face this final step with a clear plan and a level head.

That's All, Folks

Endings, whether it's the last bite of your favorite dessert or the final page of an addictive book, tend to carry a heavy emotional weight. Telling someone they're fired can feel like stepping on a LEGO brick—unexpected and painful. But sometimes it's necessary for the growth and wellbeing of everyone involved.

Remember, just because a relationship isn't working doesn't mean it's a failure. Like a funky experimental recipe, sometimes things just don't blend the way you imagined. It doesn't make the ingredients bad; they're just not right for this dish. And that's okay! Life and business are a constant dance of hellos and goodbyes, beginnings and endings.

Transitions, while they may feel daunting, are a crucial part of life and business. They open up new opportunities, lead to fresh perspectives, and often set us on the path to future success. So as you step onto this rocky terrain, remember these four steps: communicate early and often, own your part, clearly identify what you want to happen next, and agree on a separation plan.

These steps will guide you to an amicable and professional end, and remember, this is not the end. It's just the end of this chapter. Now you are well-prepared for the next exciting phase of your business journey. In fact, consider this your starting point to a brighter, more aligned future.

Case Studies: Stories of Parting Ways

Endings. They can be a bit of a bummer, can't they? But as we've discovered throughout this chapter, they can also be essential. Really, just opportunities for fresh beginnings. As we dive into the depths of parting ways, I've got a couple of real-world tales to share. Two stories about saying goodbye, from our very own business history.

Being real here, you're not likely to learn to swim by reading about swimming. But reading a few stories about how others learned to do the backstroke might give you a little more confidence before you dive in, right? That's what these case studies are all about.

We're going to pull back the curtain and give you a behind-the-scenes look at a couple of our client-expert relationships that reached the end of the road. These stories are here to show you the good, the bad, and the maybe not ugly, but definitely not-always-pretty side of how breakups can play out.

The aim is simple: to offer you a solid starting point, a foundation upon which you can start figuring out how you might handle your own business breakups. Get ready to learn from our triumphs and stumbles, so you can gracefully navigate your own parting ways. It's all part of the wild ride of business.

Case Study 1: A Story of Growing Apart
The Situation

There we were, paddling through the sea of marketing with this client. We began by crafting a brilliant marketing strategy, setting up foundational structures, and gathering assets for launch. It was all systems go, and things were looking peachy. But as we sauntered along, the client's ongoing marketing needs started resembling an exotic cuisine—something that wasn't our specialty. Basically, they craved a dish we weren't renowned for cooking.

The Plan

A huddle was necessary. The plan? To have an honest conversation with the client about the change in their marketing needs and how we might not be the best fit for this evolved trajectory. Our intention was to put their best interests at the forefront and assist in transitioning them to an expert more in sync with their peculiar taste buds.

Getting to Work

We sat down with the client, coffee in hand, and spilled the beans. Our hearts were pounding, but honesty was our policy.

We laid out our concerns, and to our relief they got it. With mutual respect, the client decided to search for a new expert. Meanwhile, we put together an epic User Guide, housing all the assets and essential information.

The Result

When the client picked their new marketing maestro, we arranged a rendezvous to hand over the baton. With the User Guide and a walkthrough of what we'd done, we passed the keys to the new expert. The client ventured into their new journey well-prepared and we tipped our hats, knowing we'd done right by them.

Lessons Learned

This adventure was a crash course in Integrity 101. We learned that:

1. Honesty is a currency that never devalues. Being upfront about our capabilities ensured the client's best interests were prioritized.

2. Bowing out gracefully is an art. Sometimes, stepping back is the most professional move.

3. Proper hand-offs are like a goodnight kiss—they leave you with a sense of completion and satisfaction.

4. Knowing your jam is essential. It's okay to admit when something is out of your wheelhouse, and there's power in recognizing your own strengths and limitations.

In the end, our hero's journey wasn't about conquering a marketing behemoth, but rather about upholding values and ensuring a fairytale ending for the client.

Case Study 2: That's Not Our Jam

The Situation

We were engaged with a client, having built their marketing strategy, established foundational elements, and put the necessary assets in place. However, as the project evolved it became evident that the ongoing marketing needs were not precisely in our area of expertise.

The Plan

Recognizing this misalignment, we planned to communicate honestly with the client about the situation. We decided to discuss their evolving needs and propose transitioning them to another expert better equipped to handle their specific requirements.

Getting to Work

During a meeting with the client, we voiced our concerns, outlining our capabilities and the limitations we had spotted. The client understood and agreed to search for a new expert. In the meantime, we compiled a comprehensive User Guide, containing all the assets and information the new expert would need.

The Result

Once the client had identified their new expert, we arranged a hand-off meeting. With the User Guide and a rundown of our work, we passed the project's reins to the client. The transition proved to be quite smooth, and the client was well-prepared to continue their journey with the new expert.

Lessons Learned

This experience taught us valuable lessons:

1. When we feel a friction, we want to address it. Being upfront about our abilities ensured the client's best interests were always in focus.

2. Hand-offs are critical for smooth transitions. Ensuring the client was well-prepared for the next phase meant they felt good about the change, and we didn't have to spend the next 60 days answering a ton of questions.

In the end, this experience underscored the importance of knowing our lane and clear communication in maintaining client relationships, even when the best course of action involves parting ways.

The Benefits of Parting Ways

It's easy to imagine the business world as a thriving metropolis, with every relationship, every connection forming a complex web of interactions. In this bustling landscape, each business and client pairing is like a unique dance, complete with its own rhythm, steps, and style. But the real trick in this dance is knowing when the music's changed, and your dance no longer fits the tune.

No business, no matter how versatile, can be the jack-of-all-trades for every client. Just as every good song must eventually end, even the most harmonious client-business relationship may reach a point where the notes start clashing. Recognizing this is the first step towards the benefits that parting ways can offer.

Often, the thought of initiating a conversation about changing directions or unaligned needs can seem as appealing as a root canal. But here's the thing: courageously voicing these concerns early on can prevent the slow deterioration of the relationship and avert potential disappointment for both parties down the line.

This openness paves the way for a smoother transition. It gives both parties a chance to reassess their current situation and find solutions or alternatives that better align with their evolving needs. It's like hitting the pause button, taking a step back, and reassessing if the dance still has the same spark. And if not, it provides the opportunity to change the tune and find a new dance partner who matches your beat.

Remember, parting ways doesn't have to be a heartbreaking ballad. It can be more of a bittersweet symphony, opening new avenues of growth, development, and opportunities for everyone involved. In essence, it's not a breakup; it's a breakthrough.

By handling these transitions with grace, professionalism, and respect, we're not just maintaining good business ethics. We're also setting ourselves up for future success, cultivating an environment that respects evolution, embraces change, and always seeks the best fit.

So, to sum it all up in a catchy chorus: parting ways can be a win-win situation. It encourages authenticity, nurtures growth, and serves as a testament to the dynamic and ever-evolving nature of business.

A Look Back Down
the Trail

*W*hat a journey we've had. You've weathered the storm and reached the summit, armed with the knowledge to navigate the world of hiring and working with experts. Kudos to you for taking this crucial step in your business growth journey.

From understanding the immense value of hiring experts, recognizing the right time to onboard them, through to the intricacies of fostering productive relationships and managing an orderly offboarding process, you've equipped yourself with a vital toolkit that's set to transform your business. You've truly embraced the power of leveraging other people's genius to propel your organization and leave a lasting impact. But remember, all of this comes with the freedom to do it your way—after all, it's your business!

Through our exploration of actionable steps to identify, recruit, and work with experts that complement your unique organizational needs, you've been empowered to extract maximum value from these relationships. Even when the road gets bumpy, you're now prepared to navigate the challenges and continue your progress confidently.

When it comes to parting ways, you now understand the significance of a well-managed offboarding process. You have the roadmap to ensure that the value delivered by your experts is retained, continuing to add to your organizational growth long after the engagement has ended. The ability to handle these transitions with grace is what will set you apart.

But hey, this is not the end of the road. Consider this a starting point, the beginning of your journey to confidently grow your support team and enhance your business. You now hold the key to unlocking an expansive world of potential and growth through effectively engaging experts. It's an exciting future, isn't it?

At HigherHelpBook.com, you'll find even more resources to guide you along the way. And you're never alone on this journey. I'm just an email away at hi@FieryFX.com. If you stumble, have a question, or even if you want to share your success stories about working with experts, don't hesitate to reach out.

In the world of entrepreneurship, nothing is more rewarding than seeing businesses grow and flourish through collaboration and the leveraging of expertise. You're poised to be a part of this vibrant ecosystem. So go forth, put these strategies to work, and watch as your business transforms in the most fantastic ways. Here's to your success!

Remember, this is just the beginning. Keep learning, keep growing and, most importantly, keep shining your unique light onto the world.

About the Author

randy Lawson has been described as a world-class explainer and a catalyst for uncovering valuable insights and distilling them into clear and effective actions. Brandy's expertise lies in identifying untapped opportunities and implementing more effective approaches in marketing and business. Her decades of experience working in the technology and software world along with her direct experience building her agency and mentoring other business owners shapes her unique perspective on the business world.

Clients and partners praise Brandy for her extraordinary insight, infectious positivity, and unwavering authenticity. With a passion for technology and an affinity for solving complex challenges, she is dedicated to shortcutting the sh*t and helping businesses thrive.

Brandy is the driving force behind FieryFX, a cutting-edge systems operations agency that helps Kitchen & Bath design businesses standardize, simplify and innovate to be more profitable & less stressful. Through her dynamic and engaging weekly podcast, "Elevated," she imparts snackable knowledge bombs on using technology, experts, and smart business to scale businesses while being humans that have enjoyable lives.

Brandy describes herself as a tech enthusiast, a lover of extravagant shoes, a pursuer of clarity, and a reforming know-it-all. Her passion for empowering companies to thrive through expert hiring and streamlined operations makes her an influential and sought-after speaker in the business world and beyond.

You can connect with or follow Brandy on the various platforms at the links below

LinkedIn - linkedin.com/in/brandylawson

Facebook - facebook.com/fieryfx

Instagram - instagram.com/fieryfx

Website - fieryfx.com

YouTube - youtube.com/@thefieryfx

Acknowledgments

Writing a book wasn't on my list of things to do in my life. But it has been a vastly rewarding experience that I will probably embark on again. It would not have been possible without these astonishing forces in my life:

My family —

> Of origin: I am one of the most fortunate people on the planet to have been born into my family. My parents have invented and reinvented themselves and their lives and bring joy to people that know them. My sisters and their families, my aunts, uncles, cousins and extended family; moments with you help shape who I want to be.

> Who chose me: My husband who supports me even when he doesn't understand, and keeps choosing us even when it means discomfort and change. Our son who makes this crazy adventure more meaningful. My team that I didn't know I needed, but without them this book, and our work, wouldn't have been possible.

My Biz Bestie: Sometimes understanding what is possible only comes into focus when you see someone else bravely scale the mountain ahead of you. Stacey, thanks for always showing me what's possible and encouraging me to try it for myself.

My communities: The Arizona WordPress community and people of uGurus who helped open my world view and gave me a space to create my next versions.

Resources

Get additional resources related to this book at

HigherHelpBook.com